Journey

OF

Truth

by Jeffry Boatright

PUBLISHED BY
SPECIAL PUBLICATIONS INC.
1999

Published by
SPECIAL PUBLICATIONS INC.
743 S.E. Fort King Street, Ocala , Florida 34471

I wish to dedicate this novel to my grandparents,

living and deceased. I shall be forever grateful of the

many wonderful memories they gave me and

stories they shared.

To
Ila Waite-Burns.
May you find joy in Journey of
truth. Discover North Florida!

Jerry S Beatty
08/19/02

Chapter 1

Amos Washington's hands were crossed as he stood propped against the cow pens peering intensely across the small pasture. Thomas Wheeler smiled as he sauntered toward Amos. Although the heat of summer was only a recent memory, Thomas wiped a bead of sweat from above his right eye.

"I guess we had better make a run into town Amos," Thomas began. "If these chickens are gonna keep laying I reckoned we're a gonna have to feed 'em."

"What about that piece of tin for the barn?" Amos asked.

"We'll get it while we're up there." Thomas announced. "We also gonna get us one of them there bird sandwiches from Miss Ruby's you always talkin about," he added.

"Get it with what?" Amos demanded.

Reaching into his overall bib and pulling out three dollars Thomas boasted, "With this."

"Where in the world did you come up with three dollars, Mr. Thomas?" Amos asked.

"I broke the Captain's horse. But don't tell Ma," Thomas instructed.

Thomas removed his small brimmed felt hat, replaced it further back over his light brown hair, and smiled mischievously at Amos. Indeed the smile was of mischief but it also offered a hint of confidence.

"I've told you 'bout flirtin' with danger now," Amos warned Thomas as he shook his finger. "You's a gonna listen to Ole Amos one of these days. Just listen to what I tell ya."

The man and boy boarded a thirty-nine Chevrolet truck and headed to Live Oak. It would be at least thirty minutes into town. The Wheelers lived about fifteen miles south west of Live Oak, the county seat of Suwannee County, Florida.

The Wheeler home was not fancy. It was however of plenty size and very functional. It sat on the remaining forty acres of the six hundred forty acre place Thomas' grandparents homesteaded and acquired through purchase.

"You want to let's go by Uncle Jack's?" Thomas asked Amos as they got onto the sandy grade that would lead the man and boy away from the Suwannee River.

Amos looked at Jack with disapproval. Amos was a black gentleman with gray hair. He believed to be around sixty two-years of age but still had the strength of a thirty year old. The faded overalls he wore always carried a pipe, smoking tobacco, and a plug of Days Work chewing tobacco. For thirty-five years, Amos Washington had worked for Thomas Wheeler's family and lived on their place. In fact, Amos was considered family.

In his trademark authoritative voice Amos asked, "Now why do you want to go by Mr. Jack's for? "We ain't a gonna stop and besides Mr. Jack don't want to be a fooled up with us."

No more was said. Amos and Thomas were both men of few words, so to speak. Although Thomas was only fourteen years of age, he fit the criteria of being a man. He was responsible, hardworking, and deemed it his responsibility to see after the place and his family while his father was serving America during World War II. Although there was little horseplay in the lad, Thomas would usually sport a mischievous smile.

Finally Thomas and Amos reached the North Florida town of Live Oak. Their first stop was Miss Ruby's Bar B Que. After devouring a bird sandwich each, they headed on over to Guthrie's Farm Supply. There they could find chicken feed and roofing tin.

Guthrie's was located next to the railroad track in Live Oak. Although it had a large area for feed, fertilizer, lumber, and seed behind the store, there was but a single drive gate accessing the large area.

Due to excessive customers that day, the parking area of Guthrie's had been filled, forcing Thomas to park inside the drive gate where the bagged feed was customarily loaded.

Amos and Thomas got out of the Chevrolet truck. Thomas went in to place his order while Amos lit his pipe and made small talk with Willie Boy Jones who was loading the laying mash in advance.

Inside, Thomas found a few familiar faces as he made way to the order counter.

"What can I get you today, Thomas?" The clerk asked.

"A couple of sheets of that tin out there and I reckoned about eight bags of laying mash for the chickens," Thomas replied with his typical grin.

The clerk started writing a charge ticket for Thomas as the other gentlemen discussed hopes of the war ending.

"Thomas," the clerk began, "any word yet from your pa?"

There was a change in the smile of Thomas. That smile of mischief was transposed to a smile of sadness. "No sir, not yet."

Suddenly the front door busted open and Horace Brooker entered. Horace looked extremely mad as his cold eyes tuned into the young Thomas Wheeler. As he began to point at Thomas the clerk recognized something was not quite right.

"What can I do for you, Mr. Brooker?" The clerk asked.

"That boy, oh that boy," Brooker's voice trembled. "He came up and parked right in my way. I'm needing to get feed and his colored fellow claims he can't drive the truck. Well I don't think this little imbecile should be driving either."

The clerk put down his tablet and started to speak, "I think it was just an oversight now Mr. Broo......"

"Feeble-mindedness!" Brooker yelled.

"I'll move the truck now, Mr. Brooker," Thomas offered as he began walking to the door.

"You doggoned right you will," Brooker said. "Now get!"

Thomas stopped immediately and turned toward the angry man. The boy was no longer smiling as he stared for just a brief moment deep into the man's eyes. "I have heard all I care to hear from you, Mr. Brooker."

Brooker then advanced Thomas as he said, "I'm going to teach you some respect boy."

As the angry Brooker drew his hand back, Amos Washington grabbed a hold to it.

In a low voice that would intimidate any man Amos said, "Touch the boy and I'll kill you. Do you understand?"

"I understand," Brooker said as Amos administered pain to him.

Amos then released Thomas' would be assailant and began walking toward Thomas when he saw the boy swiftly pull his pistol.

"Put it down or I'll shoot you," Thomas warned.

Amos turned to face Brooker and saw the man had drawn a fire stoker from display to use on the back of Amos' head. No one spoke as Amos and Thomas walked out of Guthrie's.

As they pulled out onto the highway, Amos began contemplating what had just occurred.

"Thank you," Amos said.

"Thank you," replied Thomas. "He got pretty steamed back there."

"Aw he'll get past it," Amos said.

The smile of mischief returned to young Thomas Wheeler as Amos gave him a wink of approval.

"Hey Amos," Thomas began as they approached Mason's General Store, "what do you say we stop here and get ourselves an RC Cola and a Moonpie."

"I'll buy," Amos said as Thomas wheeled the Chevrolet into the store's parking lot.

Mason's had always been one of Thomas' favorite places. He remembered his infatuation with the shiny new toys along the north wall of Mason's not so many years prior. It was at Mason's that Thomas later got his shotgun. Above all it was a friendly place to go. Mr. and Mrs. Mason, he thought seemed so fitted for their business. Of course the ever presence of their daughter, Penelope was another good reason for the young Mr. Wheeler to make an occasional purchase at the handy general store.

"Hello Mr. Mason, hello Mrs. Mason," Thomas said. "Me and ole Amos here sure would like to get a soda water and a Moonpie."

The Masons smiled at each other as Mr. Mason winked at Mrs. Mason and wiped his hands on the red apron he wore.

"Coming right up Thomas," Mr. Mason said.

"Penelope!" Mrs. Mason yelled. "Thomas is here."

"Amos, you doing all right today?" Mr. Mason asked.

"Doin' just fine, thank you," Amos responded.

"How is Rose doing Thomas?" Mrs. Mason asked.

"Oh, I guess Ma is doing pretty good Mrs. Mason. Every thing is going to be just fine you know," replied the young man.

"Well I know she is beside herself about your father," Mrs. Mason added.

"As I said," Thomas reiterated, "everything is going to be just fine ma'am."

Mr. Mason handed the young man his R.C. Cola and Thomas began chugging it down. As he brought the bottle back down, Thomas saw Penelope standing before him.

"Hey Thomas," she said.

"Well hello Miss Penelope," Thomas began. "And just how is the world treating you today?"

Penelope had no time to respond before the sheriff's deputy opened the front door and invited Amos and Thomas out for a word in private.

"The sheriff would like to have a word with you two," the deputy advised outside. "He's waiting down at the office."

"We'll do," Thomas said and once again he and Amos were climbing aboard the thirty-nine Chevrolet.

The Sheriff's Office was located in the Suwannee County Courthouse so they were only a couple of blocks away.

"I expect Sheriff Green wants to have a word with us about our little run in with Horace Brooker," Amos speculated.

"He ought to know how Horace Brooker is," Thomas replied.

"Oh he does," Amos agreed. "He just ain't used to seein' nobody stand up to 'em."

The unlikely pair chuckled conservatively as Thomas parked the truck in front of the courthouse and in they went. Sheriff Green was reviewing the weekly paper as Amos tapped upon his door.

"Please come in," the sheriff said.

The gentlemen exchanged handshakes and were seated. Sheriff Green was behind his desk with Amos and Thomas facing him.

"What happened down at Guthrie's?" The sheriff asked.

Amos and Thomas gave an accurate detail of the entire incident. They neither added to nor took anything away from their unfortunate encounter. When they were finished, the sheriff nodded steadily as if he was searching for words to say.

"That's how I heard it happened," the sheriff said. He then began to chuckle. "I guess Ole Horace is having another bad day."

"Yes sir," Amos and Thomas said simultaneously.

"Now, Thomas," Sheriff Green said, "this don't mean you can just go pulling your gun on people. Why are you carrying a gun in town anyway?"

"Well sir," Thomas began with a smile, "me and Amos here was doing some heavy duty cleaning around the place today and you know every rattler around is looking for a good place to winter. Seeing how I had my coat on over these here overalls, I just forgot I was carrying it until I walked into Guthrie's. But to be perfectly honest, I was glad."

"Good enough," said the sheriff.

Amos and Thomas were prepared to dismiss themselves when Sheriff Green asked to speak with Thomas in private. Amos showed himself to the door and the younger of the two sat back down.

"Anything on your pa?" The sheriff asked.

"Not yet," Thomas replied.

"How's your mama?" Green probed.

"Managing," answered Thomas.

Bill Green leaned back and gazed out the window. He was in his final term of office and looking forward to other problems to solve such as deciding to fish for bream or catfish. Bill had served Suwannee County well over the years and continued to do so just as he was doing at the moment.

"I am afraid I have some news that may not be so good Thomas," Bill said softly.

Thomas rose to his feet and felt his heart pound for the young man had stood his fair share of bad news. "Tell me like it is sheriff," he said.

"Now just set back down Thomas," Bill said. "Do you remember a fellow named Scott Pierce?"

"The one Pa testified against," Thomas replied while nodding his head.

"That's the one," Sheriff Green confirmed. "He got out of prison yesterday and I understand he's moving back out there by ya'll, son."

"Do you think there's going to be trouble?" Thomas Wheeler asked of the sheriff.

Bill Green lit a cigarette, blew out the match, and inhaled the cigarette smoke deeply. "I don't know," he said, "but if there is any trouble I expect you and Amos and your ma to let me handle it."

"O.K.," Thomas replied.

"I mean it," Bill said. "That is what they pay me for, Thomas. Fair enough?"

"Fair enough," said the young man as he stood up and shook Bill Green's hand.

"You see your Uncle Jack much?" The good sheriff asked.

"Not much," Thomas remarked and turned toward the door.

As Thomas walked to the door, Bill saw much of Thomas' uncle, Jack McKinley in him. Content, Bill Green completed his smoke as Thomas walked back out to Amos and the thirty-nine Chevrolet.

Chapter II

"**W**ell, it looks like we got back the same day we left," Thomas said to Amos as he turned the Chevrolet truck back into the lane leading up to the Wheeler home.

Large pecan trees stood along the lane that found it's way back to the house that Rose McKinley Wheeler had grown up in. For the first time, Thomas glanced up at the trees he had once hated, so in hopes of finding a good crop of pecans. Picking up pecans had not been one of the young man's favorite childhood pastimes, but he had come to realize the need of extra cash just for his family's survival. Thomas' father's service check had been arriving each month but it simply wasn't enough to keep everything going and everyone fed.

Rose McKinley Wheeler was indeed an adamant lady. She had not always been that way but turns of events had perhaps forced her into such rigidity. Although Amos and Thomas didn't really need her strong supervision, she often felt they did. Rose had decided the illustrious duo would spend that particular afternoon weeding out fence rows about the place. Thomas on the other hand had developed other plans. The weather was cooling and firewood sales were up, therefore Amos and he planned to journey into the river woods and gather firewood instead.

"Amos," Thomas suggested, "I'll unload the tin and feed if you'll sharpen the axes."

"We'll do," Amos replied and the two busied themselves.

Amos positioned himself on the tailgate of the truck sharpening the axes. As Thomas unloaded the feed bag by bag, they exchanged small talk. Finally, there was one bag of feed left. As Thomas grabbed the final bag of feed, he sat it back down, looked at Amos, and tilted back his hat.

"What's on your mind?" Amos asked.

"How do you deal with problems?" The young man earnestly asked.

At that moment, Amos laid the ax into the back of the truck and sat down on the tailgate. He lit his pipe, began puffing away and looked into Thomas' eyes. "Sometimes, boy, you just gots to rely on other folks for help. Folks might as well say you a grown man now, Mr. Thomas." Amos then paused and looked down at the ground before continuing. "But I know something's a botherin' you and I'll be glad to talk to you if'n you'd like. You sure is an awful young man to have so much responsibility sittin' up there on them shoulders of yours."

"Are you about ready to go get firewood?" Thomas asked Amos.

"Might as well," responded Amos. "But I thought your ma wanted us to weed out them there fence rows."

Again, a mischievous smile overtook the young man's face. "I'll handle Ma," Thomas said confidently. "You just get yourself ready to go."

As Thomas entered the kitchen from the east door leading from the outside, he found his mother inside the kitchen. The print dress she wore was quite simple and her auburn hair fell about her shoulders. Softly, she hummed Rock of Ages as Thomas went unnoticed for a short while.

"Where have you and Amos been?" Rose demanded.

"We had to go into Live Oak to get tin and chicken feed," Thomas admitted.

Rose made no comment for a moment as she continued working the flour and milk for the evening's biscuits. She did not look up at Thomas until her silence finally broke.

"I wish you would have at least let me know you were going into Live Oak," Rose sternly said. "Now I am going to have to send you back tomorrow. We are all but out of flour and sugar."

Thomas made his way to the stove and poured himself a cup of coffee for the short break. He then stared out the window as Rose continued her work.

"Why don't you go into town with me tomorrow?" Thomas asked of his mother. "Everyone is asking how you are and besides, Amos can handle things here."

Rose turned to Thomas and sighed. "Just like that," she began, "just haul off and go into Live Oak because people are asking how I am. Good Lord child, there is work to be done."

Thomas smiled as he took a sip of the piping hot coffee. "Well," he slowly began. "I just kind of thought we could swing by and check up on Uncle Jack."

Rose McKinley Wheeler suddenly stood straight as a Private might at the presence of a Colonel. "Jack," she retorted, "have you seen Jack lately?" Rose then asked Thomas.

"No ma'am," Thomas defensively replied. "I just thought maybe we could just go by and see him. I'm sure he would like to...."

Journey of Truth

"I am quite sure, young man, that if my brother would like to see us he would sober up long enough to come by and see to our well being," Rose said sharply.

"Why does he drink so much?" Thomas then probed.

Rose Wheeler then sat opposite Thomas in a straight chair and propped her elbows upon the table. Thomas then became very saddened when he saw the tears begin to form in his mother's eyes.

"I'm sorry Ma," Thomas said. "I shouldn't have...."

"It's O.K.," replied Rose. "Do you remember when Stella left?"

"Yes ma'am," Thomas said, "I reckoned Uncle Jack figured she would come back and she didn't."

"But do you know where Stella went?" Rose then asked.

"No ma'am," replied Thomas. "Where did she go?"

"Stella went to a mental hospital in Chatahoochee son," explained Rose. "Their baby died at birth and Stella never was the same. The doctors told Jack that maybe she could recover there. Of course, Jack has never been the same either. Shortly after all of that, something else really bad happened and your Uncle Jack just turned the rest of the world away."

Rose's tears had began to trickle at that point and Thomas chose to end the conversation that was pulling his mother down. He stood up and sat his cup on the kitchen table.

"Ma," Thomas began, "I won't mention it again. Just fix a list of what you need from town and I'll go after it."

Thomas Wheeler journeyed outside to rejoin his cohort, Amos. The thought had crossed the young man's mind of telling his mother of the return of Scott Pierce. He thought the better of it, however, due to the fact he did not want his mother worried any more than she had to be. Furthermore, she may ask as to why he had spoken with Sheriff Green. Thomas wasn't the kind of young man to hide things from his mother but felt she had enough going on in her mind without added frustration.

As the young man approached the barn, he removed his hat, ran his fingers through his light brown hair and gently sat the hat back upon his head. "Amos," he said with a smile, "let's get set to go to the river woods."

"What did Miss Rose say about us cuttin' firewood instead of weedin' out them there fence rows?" Amos skeptically asked Thomas.

The smile of mischief returned to the young Mr. Wheeler's face as he stated, "I guess I forgot to mention that."

As the duo prepared to board the Chevrolet truck, Thomas heard the rattle of the mail truck coming down the road. Quickly, he ran toward the mailbox to meet J.G. Phillips. J.G. was the rural route carrier and did an outstanding job with his duties giving the many barriers he may face time to time. Through his years of carrying mail, J.G. had happened up on a woman in labor, ailing livestock, long-winded preachers, and passed out drunks just to name a few delays he had experienced.

When the thirty-nine Ford the postman drove rolled to a stop, Thomas rested his foot upon the running board and smiled in at the trusted mailman.

"What you got there J.G.?" Thomas asked excitedly.

"I am doing just fine, Thomas, and how are you today?" J.G. replied with a smile.

Thomas chuckled and replied, "O.K. I get the drift J.G., now what do you have?"

J.G. sighed and began, "I'm sorry Thomas. Nothing here from your pa, just a letter from the folks down at the Bay."

Thomas' big smile shrank to a small one as he looked down at the ground. "I reckon we'll hear something sooner or later," he said.

"How's your ma dealing with it Thomas?" J.G. asked the lad.

"Good days and bad," Thomas replied. "I reckoned me and Ole Amos are fixing to go and get some firewood."

Thomas started toward the truck as J.G. sat and watched the young man. J.G. was amazed at the rapid maturity he had witnessed in Thomas. It had not been that long since J.G. had seen the proud look on the face of Charles and Rose Wheeler when they had learned that Rose was pregnant with Thomas.

"Hey Thomas," J.G. called out.

Turning and facing J.G. Thomas replied, "Yes sir?"

"Don't worry," J.G. yelled. "Old Hitler ain't got enough Germans to do your pa in and you got my word on that."

"Yes sir," Thomas called out as J.G. drove away.

J.G.'s words offered a bit of assurance for Thomas as he boarded the Chevrolet and drove off into the river woods with Amos.

Chapter III

The early morning air was a bit crisp to Thomas as he walked the bucket full of warm milk in to the detached kitchen. Upon setting it on the table, he poured himself a cup of coffee and journeyed to the living room fireplace. After warming his chilled hands, Thomas threw another log upon the fire.

"It's a bit cool out this morning," Thomas commented to his mother as he walked back into the kitchen and began sipping the coffee.

"I have that list together for you," she said. "Why don't you drop Allen and Nancy off at the school on your way to town."

"Yes ma'am," Thomas replied.

Limited conversation was normal in the Wheeler home during such early hours. When the younger children would wake however, talk was sure to increase. Nancy was six and Allen was five. Nancy's primary duties were assisting Rose in the house and Allen assumed the duties of feeding the livestock in the evening or anything else Thomas might ask of him. Allen and Nancy were required to complete all school assignments though prior to their home chores each day.

Thomas woke his younger siblings and went out to the old bunk house where Amos awaited him with a cup of coffee. It was a morning ritual for Thomas to join Amos for coffee. There they would discuss the day ahead and compare their dreams from the night prior. It was never said but Thomas was mainly just checking on Amos.

That particular morning Thomas reminded Amos of his intent to go into Live Oak and Amos declined the offer to ride along.

"I expect I best be workin' on Miss Rose's fence rows Thomas," Amos explained. "An' I might just stroll down to the river come 'bout lunch time an' catch us a mess of them there catfish."

"I might just make it back in time to join you then," Thomas warned with a grin.

Back in the house, Thomas found his young brother and sister working away at the grits, eggs, sausage, gravy, and biscuits their mother had prepared.

"Thomas Wheeler," Rose called out, "you get on back as soon as you can so that you may work on those fence rows you and Amos avoided so well yesterday."

"Yes ma'am," Thomas replied as he smiled and winked at the two younger Wheelers.

"I bet he goes and sees that Penelope Mason," Allen blurted.

"I might do just that if she weren't in school today," Thomas boasted.

"Why don't you go to school Thomas?" Nancy asked her older brother.

As Rose walked toward the table she wiped her hands and looked quite pitiful at Nancy. "He is going back Nancy," Rose said, "just as soon as Papa gets back. Thomas is going back to school."

"Why can't he go now?" Nancy further probed.

"Because," Rose candidly explained, "right now Thomas is having to help make enough money for us to live on. Things will get better though, don't you worry."

After dropping Allen and Nancy off at the country school approximately one and one half miles north of the Wheeler home, Thomas followed along the river to his Uncle Jack's cabin. The little cabin was probably another mile and a half from the school. It set off the road a couple of hundred yards and looked down over the river. There was no landscape, just woods.

Sure enough, Jack's thirty-four Ford coupe was parked out front. Thomas smiled a bit and rolled to a stop right behind his uncle's car. Judging by the leaves atop Jack's coupe, Thomas figured his uncle had not driven anywhere in a few days. Outside the house appeared abandoned as the young man found no evidence of routine chores and yard maintenance.

After a few moments of contemplation, Thomas placed the Chevrolet truck in reverse and backed out. He had no idea what to say to Jack so there was no reason to stay. Therefore, he drove on into Live Oak.

As Thomas rode into town, he couldn't help but wonder about his sudden interest in Jack. They had never been around each other all that much, Thomas realized. Although the young man was but fourteen years of age and feared nothing or no one, he was not without intelligence either. Perhaps Thomas would feel less threatened by Scott Pierce and his entourage of undesirable characters with Jack's presence. Nonetheless, Thomas was confident Jack would be far from beneficial to him.

In town, Thomas found little traffic. The crop season had ended and folks were at their places preparing for the winter months ahead. Upon rolling the Chevrolet truck to a complete stop, Thomas began a short walk over to Mason's General Store. Next to Mason's was Earl Tucker's barber shop. Outside Earl's barber shop were four rocking chairs. The chairs had been placed there so that Earl's awaiting patrons may enjoy the outdoors until he could finish his story or at least get to a stopping point and cut their hair.

In deep thought, Thomas walked toward Mason's as he thought of his missing father until suddenly he heard someone call out, "Hey kid." It was Scott Pierce.

Thomas knew who he was because he had seen Pierce's picture before. Besides, he remembered Pierce before he was sent to prison.

"What do you want?" Thomas asked candidly.

"I want your pa," Pierce frankly replied with a couple of his friends standing on either side of him.

"My pa is at war," stated the young man. "I reckon you'll just have to wait."

"Maybe I won't," Pierce said as he looked deep into the boys eyes. Scott Pierce then began laughing as he stood from the rocking chair and said, "Tell your folks I'm back, little boy!"

Even at fourteen, Thomas Wheeler had been stared in the eyes by some of the worst of men but Scott Pierce was different and Thomas was smart enough to know it. His stare was cold and hard while his laughter was unkind. Thomas remained quiet as he turned to walk away. Each step he heard the beat of his own heart. It was slow and sadistic sounding and with each beat, the young man became more angry. He quietly told himself, "Keep walking Thomas Wheeler, keep on walking."

"So I reckon you call yourself the man of the family now," Pierce called out and laughed. "I aim to find out how big of a man you are."

Thomas had gone through much in his short years. His family had struggled financially, his pa had gone to war and was now missing. That particular moment however was just about the breaking point for the young man.

No matter how badly Thomas Wheeler wanted to charge Scott Pierce with all his might and fight for his family, the young man continued walking with his heart filled with a malice he had never felt before.

Thomas continued his steady pace toward Mason's Store. There he would find friendly faces and there he would again face questions about his missing father. Prior to that moment, the young man had been able to address such questions with his trademark smile. He was however unable to do so after the less than pleasant encounter with Scott Pierce.

After completing his business, Thomas started toward the front door when Mr. Mason called out. "Thomas," Mr. Mason said.

"Yes sir?" replied the young man.

"Your Uncle Jack, how is he Thomas?" Mr. Mason asked.

"He's all right I reckon," Thomas began. "He doesn't leave home too much you know."

Mr. Mason smiled as he walked toward Thomas Wheeler and sat down on a wooden crate. "Did I ever tell you about the time your Uncle Jack probably saved my life?" He asked the young man.

"No sir," replied Thomas, "not that I recall."

"Well he did," Mr. Mason began while maintaining his smile. "Let's see now, it must have been about sixteen years ago. We were all out at Old Man Logan's place. Mr. Logan was cooking off a batch of his medicine when a couple of fellows from Madison County came across the river to get some and stay overnight to enjoy the festivities that were sure to come."

Thomas listened intently as Mr. Mason began his story. The store owner lit his pipe and Thomas also sat on a wooden crate. As the young man situated his purchased items on the floor next to the crate, Mrs. Mason walked by and smiled in satisfaction. It indeed did her good to see her husband take up time with Thomas. She had much compassion in her heart for the young man and his family.

"Well what happened?" Thomas asked with the return of his trademark smile.

"We were all just gathered around Mr. Logan's still and these two fellows were feeling no pain. There were a few people trying to play music on guitars, fiddles, and banjos when they started staring at me a lot and decided I had somehow done them an unjust over in Madison County," Mr. Mason explained.

"You?" Thomas asked in disbelief.

"Ain't it the craziest thing you ever heard of Thomas," Mason responded. "Well anyhow I decided to just leave and ride north toward the house where I should have been all along. We were all riding horses and little did I know those two Madison County fellows had followed me out from Old Man Logan's."

Thomas continued listening as Mr. Mason described the river woods on that full moon summer night around 1930. While the man talked and the boy listened, Mrs. Mason carried the two a cup of coffee each.

"Did they slip up on you?" Thomas asked.

"They did indeed," Mason chuckled. "Before I knew it, they had eased right up behind me. Oh, I heard them about one hundred paces back but I didn't run for it. They were probably gonna catch me anyway and I didn't want to cause my horse to get hurt too, so I just stopped and waited. It was a bit of an open spot just before an old head of oak trees where the road bends north of Mr. Logan's place."

"I know right where you talkin' about," interrupted Thomas.

"Sure enough those two fellows decided they were gonna work me over just for good measure so we all got off our horses," Mr. Mason continued. "The first one knocked me down and I came up madder than an old wet settin' hen. Well then the second one grabbed me

Journey of Truth

from behind so he could hold me while the first one beat on me. It was just about then somebody eased around that bend in the road on a horse headin' south and it was your Uncle Jack. With the old moon givin' up plenty of light Jack saw what was about to take place."

Sarah Mason had heard this story many times before. Each time she would hear the story, she too would listen intently as if it were her first time. She and Paul Mason were courting one another when the whole thing happened. One might think she would have been angered in hearing such a story but instead she was moved each time she heard it. It was yet another story about a local hero, a man named Jack McKinley.

"What did Jack do?" Thomas Wheeler asked prior to taking another sip of coffee.

Mason's smile then diminished as he continued with the story. "Your Uncle Jack rode right up there with a smile and stopped his horse beside us. He asked those fellows if there was room for him to join the party. When they told him it wasn't none of his affair, Jack asked what I had done. They told 'em they was pretty sure I had shot up their brother's bar over in Madison County. Well Jack just started laughing as he slumped over his saddle horn and looked down on us. He told those strangers there was no way I could have done it because he had. Of course neither one of us had done it but that's what Jack told 'em."

"Uncle Jack fight 'em?" Thomas asked Mr. Mason.

"No," Mason replied. "After telling them that, he told 'em they could go and tell their brother that Jack McKinley was the man that shot up his bar."

"And the two men rode off in a trot," Sarah Mason added. "More coffee Thomas?"

"No ma'am," the young man answered. "I guess I had best be gettin' back toward home now.

As Thomas walked outside the general store, Mrs. Mason commented to her husband, "Jack couldn't have had a son more like him could he have dear."

Mr. Mason agreed.

Chapter IV

Upon returning to the farm, Thomas carried in the things he had purchased for his mother in town. Carefully he placed each of the items in their respective places. Rose Wheeler had cooked some peanut candy and was at the time in the pantry retrieving jars of vegetables for the evening meal. The Wheelers called this meal supper. Since Miss Rose was away from the kitchen, Thomas helped himself to some of the cooling candy.

The young man then fixed four peanut butter sandwiches and packed them in a basket. He also grabbed a couple of apples and was on his way out to meet his ever ready partner, Amos.

"Amos," Thomas yelled.

"Yes sir, Mr. Thomas, right here," Amos replied.

Thomas sauntered over to Amos and looked over his shoulders. He then smiled at the old farm hand as he reached into the bib of his overalls. "Here," Thomas said, "Mama just made it."

Amos looked with a degree of disapproval at Thomas. He did however take the peanut candy and reply, "Boy, your ma gonna get both of us."

"Well she will just have to do that later," Thomas replied. "We need to go down to the river and get a couple of cords of firewood. While in town, I made a sale. It'll help with groceries."

"What about them fence rows?" Amos then asked.

"They don't buy groceries," Thomas replied earnestly.

Amos and Thomas then loaded the truck with axes, a cross cut saw and plenty of rope. They were ready to make an afternoon of work. As they drove off, Thomas decided to check the sweet potatoes that adjoined the Pierce property. They were ready to dig, Amos advised the young farmer.

As the two discussed plans of digging the potatoes, Thomas peered across at the home of Scott Pierce. He saw movement there and was reminded of the words Pierce had said so harshly earlier in the day. Amos detected a change in the mood of his young protege.

"What's on your mind Thomas?" Amos asked.

"Nothing," replied the young man as he continued to gaze across the Pierce property. "Nothing at all."

"I see that Pierce fellow's came home," Amos said.

"Yes sir," Thomas responded as he angrily tossed a stick over onto Pierce land.

The story Mr. Mason had shared with Thomas about Jack McKinley continued to weigh heavy on the lad's mind. Suddenly Thomas realized his answer to the threats of Scott Pierce just might be his Uncle Jack.

"Tell me about Uncle Jack," Thomas suggested.

Amos took his pipe from his overalls, lit it and began puffing. He then looked at Thomas. "Look across there boy," Amos instructed as he pointed about the adjoining six hundred acres of land. "That is partly the problem of your Uncle Jack."

"He don't like it that Grandpa sold it?" Thomas asked.

"Your Grandpa didn't sell the land," Amos said sadly.

"What are you saying?" Thomas then inquired.

"Your Uncle Warren lost the place in a poker game with old man Pierce," Amos abruptly informed Thomas.

Thomas began breathing hard as he glanced back and forth at Amos and the land. "What do you mean he lost it in a poker game?" Thomas demanded. "It wasn't his to gamble."

"Well, I reckon it wasn't all his," Amos admitted, "but he sure 'nough gambled it away."

Thomas remained quiet for a brief period. He stared at the ground and then looked across a portion of the six hundred acres his younger uncle had lost in a game of cards. Soon he looked at Amos and said, "Well the bet should never have stood seeing how the whole place wasn't his to gamble."

"Dat's right," Amos replied, "you gotta remember boy that word called honor. Now Mr. nor Mrs. McKinley neither one likes what happened but they knowed Mr. Warren's bet had to be honored. 'Sides, Pierce and his men would have got it somehow and it's better to give up land than life."

Again, the two set quietly on the tailgate of the Chevrolet truck. After a very short while, Amos picked the ax back up to reconvene his wood cutting duties

"Your Grandpa McKinley was a gonna deed me forty acres on the back corner," Amos said with a grin. "Now couldn't you just see Ole Amos bein' a land owner?"

"So that's why Uncle Jack's been so sore for so long?" Thomas asked verbosely.

As Amos rubbed his thumb across the edge of the ax, he began to speak, "I don't know. And even if I did know, it ain't my place to be telling you about Jack. Why don't you ask your ma?"

Thomas made no response. He and Amos journeyed on out into the river woods where the two worked diligently that afternoon chopping wood to sell. While working, Thomas and Amos discussed plans of transporting the soon to be dug sweet potatoes to a market in Jacksonville.

Finally break time came and the two men devoured the peanut butter sandwiches Thomas had prepared earlier in the day. While eating the sandwiches, the young man observed two squirrels at play. They would chase one another back and forth and Thomas found it pleasing to see two creatures free of fear and concern.

"I'll go and get the shotgun," Amos began. "We can have us some squirrel stew."

"Leave them be," pleaded Thomas. "They're having too much fun."

"Lawd child what's gotten into you lately?" Amos exclaimed.

"Aw we don't really need that meat Amos," Thomas said. "Ma's got a smokehouse full of meats at home. Besides, we both gonna be too tired to clean 'em anyhow."

Amos smiled and resumed his duties of wood chopping while Thomas began loading the chopped wood. Toward the end of the day, the two men had accumulated two cords of firewood and drove back to the Wheeler farm.

They both washed up and Amos went out to his quarters as Thomas went into the Wheeler home. While walking toward the back door, he seized the ball his siblings were intensely playing with, only to tease them. Upon giving it back, Thomas entered the back door.

Inside, Rose awaited Thomas' return and greeted her dedicated son with a piping hot cup of coffee. The aroma of fresh sausage had absorbed the kitchen she was working in so diligently.

"I would offer you some peanut candy," Rose said with a slight grin, "but I think you might have already helped yourself."

"It was good," replied the young man as he was unable to muster up a better defense on such short notice.

Thomas found his mother to be in a cheerful mood that evening. Upon explaining why the fence rows did not get weeded out, Rose offered her approval. She was pleased with the small sale of firewood.

"What would you think about us going down to the bay and stay a spell until your pa comes home?" Rose asked her oldest son out of the clear blue.

Thomas was not at all receptive to the idea but handled it as diplomatically as possible. His trademark smile withered away as he tipped his hat back and looked at his mother.

"I thought you didn't care too much for Uncle Warren," Thomas said.

"He is my brother," Rose replied.

"Jack is your brother too," Thomas snapped back.

"Warren might have gambled away the farm but at least he didn't abandon his family," Rose said. "I shouldn't have said that about gambling away the farm," she sighed. "That's something we never told you about."

"Amos told me," Thomas replied softly.

"It wasn't his place to tell," Rose scorned. "I have a good a min............"

"I asked him. The decision I plainly understand is yours to make," the young man began. "But I should certainly hope we can stay here."

"But I thought you liked the coast," Rose said as she sat down opposite the table from Thomas.

"Oh I do," he replied. "But Ma, we have our own place to see after and what about Amos? Just who is going to see after him."

"I think Amos is capable of seeing after himself and besides he can take care of the place while we're away. Maybe you can even get back into school," suggested Rose.

"What about Jack?" Thomas asked.

"What about him?" Rose responded scornfully.

"I just think maybe we ought to be seeing after him too," Thomas argued.

Rose returned to the stove where she was melting butter and began stirring. "It doesn't appear that your uncle Jack cares all that much about our well being now does it?" She replied.

Thomas realized it best to remain on the place for he knew Pierce would burn them out if they left. In fact, he was pretty sure the villain would do just the same if they stayed. He had heard the Jack McKinley stories though. That was his hope. Thomas realized if only he could help Jack return to normal, Pierce would be sure to back down from famous Jack McKinley. The problem that seemed to persist for Thomas however was that he could not allow his mother to learn of the threats made by Pierce.

"What was Jack like when ya'll were young ma?" Thomas asked softly.

Rose then began to smile. "He was like a legend around these parts," she said. "He could be as rough as a bull or as gentle as a mourning dove, that was Jack. I remember one time your grandma was sick and Jack had been working cows with Pa. When Jack got in, he neither slept nor ate. He stayed up all night with Ma and come morning, he had picked a hand full of phlox for her. You know Ma loves phlox so. That same day he learned the man at a place called Garvey's, that used to tailor clothes here, had been rude to me and made me cry. Well Jack just went up there and brought that fellow out here and made him apologize to me. Quite a character your uncle Jack was, quite a character."

Thomas chuckled as he pictured his uncle escorting the Dress Maker out to apologize to his mother. "You mean he brought him all the way out here Ma?" Thomas asked. "I'm surprised the fellow would even come."

"Coming was better than his other choice," Rose readily admitted her brother's intent. "Jack McKinley is.....Jack McKinley was nobody to mess with."

"You think he's finished don't you ma?" Thomas asked presumptuously.

Rose looked sharply at her son. She then tossed her head back and softly bit her bottom lip. "Why can't you understand the liquor has gotten to him, Thomas? Is it so hard for you to understand?"

"Scott Pierce is back," Thomas said. He had had no intention of speaking with his mother about Pierce's return. Pierce however was across the pasture and it wasn't like he wouldn't be seen. What Thomas did refrain from telling his mother was of his encounter with Pierce in town earlier.

"I wanted to talk with you about that," Rose began. "If you see him coming, go the other way. He is a very dangerous man, Thomas. He rode over here this afternoon a wantin' to see your pa. I don't think he believes your pa ain't home either."

Thomas stared down at the table. Finally he looked up at his mother and said, "Ma, that's reason enough for us not to go to the bay."

"Do you remember the way things were before Pierce went to jail?"

"I remember," Thomas replied, "but, Ma, we have to stay and protect what we have here."

"With what?" Rose yelled. "A possible widow woman, an old black man, and a boy. Pierce will run right through us as soon as he gets ready."

"That's why we need Jack," Thomas confidently said.

"Go gather the eggs," Rose instructed Thomas.

As he departed out the back door attempting to resume his typical smile, the young man entertained his own thoughts.

Chapter V

The Wheeler family ate around six o'clock that evening. Rose had fried a mess of catfish Amos had caught. She had also made hushpuppies and baked a few sweet potatoes. The meal was one of Thomas's favorites. Of course Thomas was finding himself partial to just about anything in the line of food. It should go without saying, grits and guava jelly were also on the table.

Allen and Nancy picked at their food while Rose and Thomas ate a bit more seriously. As he ate, Thomas thought of how nice it would be to see his pa sitting at the head of the table. He was also thinking of taking a ride to Jack McKinley's cabin.

"When's Papa coming home?" Nancy asked so innocently.

Rose and Thomas looked at one another as they were at a loss of words. For so long they had spoken confidently but both knew as the days passed without word of Charles Wheeler, the least likely his homecoming would be.

"Hopefully soon," Rose said forcing a smile. "You two little ones had better eat up or I'll tell Amos you didn't like the fish."

It worked. Nancy and Allen began eating their meal as Thomas enjoyed his dessert from Columbia-Coffee.

"I reckoned I had best go down to the river and check a fish trap Amos set out yesterday," Thomas said as he enjoyed his last sip of coffee.

"Take Allen with you," suggested Rose.

"It's a pretty long walk from the road," Thomas replied quickly. "I had best go alone this time."

Rose then gave Thomas a stern look and began, "You should start spending more time with your brother young man. One day you may wish he were around a little more."

"Yes ma'am," Thomas replied with a smile as he quickly walked to the fireplace where his jacket hung."

As Thomas walked out the door, Rose called out, "Don't be late, Thomas Wheeler."

Thomas Wheeler had no intentions of going to check Amos' fish trap. He was determined to see Jack McKinley and to Jack McKinley's cabin Thomas drove. The weather was pretty cold and Thomas thought it peculiar to find no smoke drifting from the chimney when he drove up in Jack's driveway. The Ford coupe however remained in the yard.

At the door, Thomas knocked a few times but got no answer. Finally, he turned the door handle and wandered on inside. The young man recalled having been inside the cabin only once before. It was shortly after his Aunt Stella had been sent away that Thomas had gone there with his mother and Grandmother McKinley.

The cabin was not fancy but perhaps nicer than the young man had expected. Everything appeared to be in its respective place. Upon the tiny living area walls were family portraits. In fact, the place appeared to Thomas as if his aunt were still living there.

"Jack," Thomas called out. "You here Jack McKinley? This is Thomas, Thomas Wheeler."

Jack did not answer so Thomas continued calling. Slowly he meandered over to the dining room table. Atop the red and white checked tablecloth was only a half full bourbon bottle.

As Thomas walked outside, he heard music in the distant woods. He was sure no houses were to be found in that area so curiosity got the best of the lad. Instead of walking to the truck, Thomas continued by foot up river in the direction of where the music was coming. Not only was the young man hearing music, but laughter as well. He even detected the odor of oak wood burning from the same direction.

Finally Thomas stumbled up on a small wooden building standing alone among cedar trees nestled beneath large oak trees. The building was about one hundred yards away from the dirt road and perhaps an equal distance to the river. The tin roof was of a steep pitch and there were no windows, just wooden shutters that had been closed. The building was approximately twenty feet in width and forty feet in depth. It was a perfect rectangle. Toward the back of the building on the south side was a stove pipe protruding from the wall. It then made a ninety degree turn straight up. Smoke from the burning oak wood slowly drifted into the darkness of night.

For a short while, Thomas just stood and looked at the building. Something about the place fascinated him. It was perhaps the music. He found the sound a bit unusual. Thus far he had been exposed to predominately gospel music. He had also enjoyed hearing the songs of Roy Acuff and Ernest Tubb. This music was however different. It was faster and rather cheerful. There were horns blowing and he even heard an accordion. Amos referred to them as groan boxes.

It wasn't long before a black gentleman walked outside. Thomas gave a conscious effort to avoid bursting out in laughter as he watched the tanked gentleman dance and sing as he dandily snapped his long bony fingers. The suit he wore was white with a bold pinstripe. Although it was difficult for Thomas to see due to the darkness, he had gotten a close look at the man as the drunken man shuffled past the lad.

Quietly, Thomas stepped behind a tree and watched the man walk behind the building. Again, curiosity began eating at the boy as he quietly followed the black man. Thomas retreated only a short way into the woods when he realized it was an outhouse the gentleman had gone inside.

After the gentleman shuffled his way back inside the music filled building, Thomas made his own way to the front door of the place. Thomas Wheeler was an innocent lad. He was however not a naive young man. He had already realized the building was a juke joint and maybe more. What he was unclear of was three things. First of all, Thomas could not understand why a juke joint would be in the middle of nowhere like this. Secondly, he found it interesting that he had never heard of such a place. Finally, Thomas thought it to be peculiar that there was only one car around the place. A single thirty-eight Ford coupe with a caved in trunk lid was the only vehicle there.

At last, the young man turned to journey back into the woods and walk to his truck when a voice called out. "Who's out there?" Someone asked.

Slowly, Thomas turned around and said in a trembling voice, "Wheeler, I'm Thomas Wheeler."

"Well then, Thomas Wheeler," a dandy black gentleman replied. "Come in here out of the cold and I'll fix you up a cup of coffee. You do drink coffee?"

"That's O.K.," Thomas replied. "I was just on my way home. Bye now."

"Wait a minute boy," the man commanded. "Ain't you Jack McKinley's nephew?"

"Yes sir," Thomas replied.

"You want to see him?" The man at the door asked. "He's inside."

Thomas wanted to see Jack indeed. Scott Pierce was eating at Thomas and the boy was merely hoping his uncle could be of aid. Undoubtedly Pierce would not give up on making the Wheelers' life miserable unless he felt threatened. From what Thomas had heard, Jack McKinley was once the man for the job. The question at hand was could Jack McKinley still handle such a task and if he could, would he?

Slowly Thomas Wheeler made his way to the front door of the building. He was scared but chose to go inside just the same. Inside, he saw a world he had never dreamed of. The cheerful gentleman Thomas had already seen outside was apparently preparing to reconvene his music making as he held a saxophone. Along the back of the building was a small bandstand. Upon the band stand was also two other musicians. They were also dressed in the white suits with pinstriping.

Remaining focused on the bandstand, Thomas slowly walked toward the musicians. They appeared so confident in what they were doing. Thomas then recalled what Amos had told him about the clubs in which he had visited out in New Orleans. The young man thought to himself how Amos would enjoy this place too.

"Does your mother know you are here?" Asked a man from behind Thomas.

When Thomas turned around, he saw Jack McKinley. "No sir," Thomas replied.

"Good," Jack said. "She would kill you," he added with a smile.

Thomas just stared at his uncle. Jack McKinley was indeed a large man. He stood well over six feet tall and was of heavy stature. The young man's uncle had very sad eyes. Perhaps they were once charming to the ladies but Thomas found them to be sad and almost hopeless. The lad found his uncle to be well groomed. His hair was parted to the side and combed back neatly. His face was clean shaven with an obvious scar on his right cheek. Jack wore brown trousers, a white shirt, suspenders and railroad boots.

"Please join me," Jack said politely.

Thomas nodded and the two walked over to the table Jack obviously occupied daily. Thomas glanced around at his surroundings while he thought about the conversation he wanted to have with Jack. The one and only door Thomas saw faced the east. Along the south wall was a bar. There were six black gentlemen and two black ladies enjoying life as they drank merrily at the bar. Along the north wall of the building were four tables. Each table would comfortably seat four.

Much to Thomas' surprise, the building almost had a ritzy appeal to it. For lighting, chandeliers hung from the ceiling with lighted candles burning in them. Along the bar there were as many kerosene lanterns as there were on the tables. The center area of the building was actively used for a dance floor. At the time two tired couples were swaying their way across the floor as the band played My Old Dixie Flame.

Along the walls were pictures of music legends such as Cab Callaway, Louis Armstrong, Glen Miller, and Nat King Cole. Interestingly, all of the photographs had been autographed.

Jack lit a Lucky Strike cigarette and poured himself a shot of moonshine from a brown jug. He then looked at Thomas seriously.

"Nice place," Thomas said due to the lack of better words.

"What are you doing here?" Jack asked as the gentleman delivered Thomas' cup of coffee and joined them.

Thomas explained to Jack about going to his house, hearing the music, and finding the place. Meanwhile, the black gentleman seated himself at the table with the men.

"We call it The Club Palmetto," Jack said. "Only a few of us know about it. It is a secret Thomas. Can you keep a secret?"

"Yes sir," Thomas promised as he was attempting to muster the courage to talk to Jack about Scott Pierce.

"Do you know why we keep it a secret?" Jack then asked.

"Because moonshine is served here," Thomas replied boldly.

"Partly," Jack said with a smile. "look around Thomas. Everyone here is happy but everyone here has problems of their own to deal with too. Old Zeb here runs a respectable little place. We all come in here and enjoy each other and the music. For just a little while we can forget about our problems. There are never any problems here. Problem is if people started finding out about the Club Palmetto, then everybody would want to come and enjoy it. Then fights would start and Sheriff Green would have to come out and close us down."

Thomas understood and respected what Jack had told him. He swore his secrecy to Jack and Zeb. Jack downed his moonshine and finished his cigarette while Thomas sipped on the coffee Zeb had carried him.

"People don't drive here I suppose so other people won't notice the automobiles coming in and out," Thomas commented.

"You are very observant," Jack said. "Zeb is usually the only who drives here."

"Who is the band?" Thomas asked.

"Louie and The Louisiana Foghorns," Jack replied. "They are passing through on their way to a show in Tampa at some swank joint. They play all the big clubs."

Thomas couldn't help wondering what they were doing at a club nobody knew about in the middle of nowhere.

"Have any of them been here?" Thomas asked Jack as the lad pointed at the autographed photographs.

"There have been many musicians here," Jack replied.

Thomas found the music rather entertaining but too loud to converse with his uncle privately. After a few minutes, he asked Jack outright for a word in private. As any good uncle should do, Jack obliged. The two trampled through the woods over a well beaten path toward Jack's cabin. Thomas had not seen the path earlier that evening.

Chapter VI

As Thomas Wheeler and Jack McKinley made their way into Jack's cabin, just two miles south Amos was entertaining unwelcome guests. It was bound to happen. Scott Pierce and a couple of his goons had shown up near the entrance to the Wheeler farm as Amos was walking back from checking his fish traps. They were just far enough away that Rose didn't detect a thing out of the ordinary.

The past of Scott Pierce was no secret. He was a very flamboyant man who in fact would readily seek the spot light. His flamboyance was evident in his personality and attire. Much like his father, people either strongly liked or strongly disliked Pierce. Scott's father, Sam however could be a reasonable man. Scott possessed the charm of a kitten and the arrogance of a water moccasin. Prison had not changed him.

Pierce was indeed a sophisticated dresser. He was always seen wearing light colored double breasted suits that hinted a tropical look. It was said Scott Pierce owned as many as twenty of such suits prior to his incarceration. Upon being released from the state penitentiary he had each of his suits replaced. Saddle oxford shoes were also a normality in Pierce's dress code. Sometimes he would sport a fedora and times he wouldn't.

Amos Washington did not care for Scott Pierce in the least. It was evident as the two men stared into each other's eyes.

"I want Charles Wheeler," Pierce demanded as the head lights of the car shined directly on Amos.

"But I'm a tellin' ya' Mister," Amos replied angrily, "Mr. Charles ain't up there. Naw Sir, he missin' in the war."

As Amos looked into the eyes of Pierce's goons, they could see an inkling of grief in the black gentleman's expression. They also were aware of the older man's capabilities. Furthermore they realized his capabilities had kept Scott Pierce from confronting him alone.

"Look boys," Amos began, "he ain't up there. Now I'm beggin' you please leave us alone."

"Who is up there?" Pierce asked with his hideous grin.

"It's just Mrs. Wheeler, the two little chilrens an' I don't know 'bout the oldest boy," Amos replied with whatever civility he could gather.

"Will you give them a message for me?" Pierce asked subtlety.

"Yes sir," replied Amos as he appeared to relax.

Pierce looked first at the man on his right then at the one on his left. He then looked at Amos, smiled, and ordered his thugs to take care of business. They beat Amos unmercifully as Scott Pierce looked on and laughed uncontrollably.

After what they considered fit treatment, the three hoodlums left Amos Washington lying on the ground bleeding. It was truly an unnecessary act. Amos had never been anything but kind to others.

Meanwhile, Jack McKinley and Thomas Wheeler had made their way inside Jack's cabin and built a fire. Jack offered to make a pot of coffee only if Thomas was going to be there for a lengthy visit.

"I'm only here for a minute," Thomas advised. "I need to get on back to the place."

"Very well," Jack replied. "what is on your mind?"

"Scott Pierce," Thomas responded bluntly.

Jack stiffened and his sad blue eyes widened as his nephew said Pierce's name. The boy's uncle without further word commenced to scooping coffee grounds so that a pot of coffee could be made. He then lit a Lucky Strike and removed his coat. Thomas watched carefully as Jack gently removed his revolver from a leather shoulder holster and gently placed it on the table with the barrel facing the door. Finally, Jack spun around a straight table chair and sat in it backwards as he faced his nephew directly across the table.

"What about Scott Pierce?" Jack asked in a gruff voice.

"He's out of prison and living across the field from us," Thomas replied in a frightful voice.

"Why are you here telling me this?" Jack then probed.

"He don't believe my pa's a missing," Thomas admitted.

"So you have talked to Pierce?" Jack inquired.

Thomas leaned back in his chair and inhaled deeply, exhaled slowly and looked into Jack's eyes. Jack saw immense concern in the lad's eyes. The uncle was even seeing something in Thomas's eyes he had seen in his own.

"I saw him in town," Thomas said. "I know about Pa testifying and helping send Scott Pierce to jail. He wants to get back at Pa now."

Jack looked sympathetically at Thomas. The two remained silent for a brief spell until Jack broke the silence. "Did Pierce threaten you?" Jack bluntly asked Thomas.

"Pretty much," Thomas replied.

"Pretty much," Jack snapped. "either he threatened you or he didn't. Now which is it?"

Thomas was beginning to regret going to his estranged uncle with the problem. In fact, he had about decided he and Amos could handle the situation on their own. Little did he know of Amos' unfriendly encounter with Scott Pierce and company.

"I'm sorry Thomas," Jack said as he detected the lad's unease. "Do you want my help?"

Sarcastically Thomas answered, "Well I certainly wouldn't want to impose."

Jack stood and walked over to the coffee pot. He poured two tin cups of java as he laughed. "I do believe you have a helping of Rose McKinley Wheeler flowing through your veins nephew," Jack said.

"Is that a fact?" Thomas retorted.

"That is a fact indeed," said Jack. "Tell me is she still feisty as ever?"

"Ma ain't quite the same these days. Pa's missing in the war you know," stated the young man as he looked down at the table.

"No I didn't," Jack sadly replied as he attempted to sip the scorching coffee.

As Jack appeared to contemplate the consequences of Charles Wheeler's indefinite absence, Thomas reviewed his own behavior. The young man had so looked forward to speaking with Jack McKinley. He was however disappointed in himself for losing his composure. It was indeed out of character for the otherwise calm and cool Thomas Wheeler. He had planned to make such a positive impression on his uncle but now feared failure.

"Perhaps I should speak with Pierce," Jack said.

"Do you think it would help?" Thomas asked

"Can't hurt," Jack replied as he then reached for the bourbon bottle. "But first you have to share with me exactly what took place when you and Pierce saw one another."

Thomas complied with Jack's request and gave him a play by play account of his and Scott Pierce's conversation in Live Oak. Jack listened intensely as Thomas' words illustrated for him what had taken place.

Upon Thomas' completion of his narrative about the Pierce encounter, Jack got up and walked over to the pictures hanging on the wall. He looked at the one of his parents hanging up on the wall and then turned back to look at Thomas.

"Do you see your grandparents often?" Jack asked Thomas.

"Pretty often," Thomas replied.

"How are they?" Jack probed.

"O.K. I suppose," Thomas answered. "When did you see them last?"

"I guess about six months ago," Jack said. "I write them and they write me but I don't go to the bay you know."

"I know," Thomas replied. "I think they came by here a couple of weeks ago but you weren't here."

"Yea, I was probably up at the club," answered Jack.

"Are you there much?" Thomas then asked as he made his own way to the coffee pot.

"Quite a bit," Jack answered expressionless.

"Do you just go there or do you have some sort of an interest in the Club Palmetto?" Thomas asked.

"Sure is cool out," Jack replied with a smile.

Thomas knew what that meant. He had attempted to initiate conversation on a subject his uncle chose not to discuss. Therefore, Thomas would not revisit that subject for the remainder of the night.

"I suppose I just needed to get your opinion about Pierce," Thomas said to Jack. "You know you are kind of like a legend around here and I thought maybe you could give me some advice. I don't expect you to handle it for us."

Jack looked at Thomas as he sat back down in the chair. Jack knew his sister, Thomas's mother was not very happy with him. He also knew she would probably not be receptive to his help in any manner. He had spent ten years wallowing in his own pity and had failed miserably at being a big brother to his sister.

"What about your mother? Does she know you are talking with me?" Jack asked Thomas.

"No sir," replied the lad. "I haven't told her about the problems with Scott Pierce. She already has enough on her mind."

"O.K.," Jack said. "Come by and pick me up around ten or eleven in the morning and let's you and me take little ride and I'll have a word with Mr. Scott Pierce. Then I will have a word with Mrs. Rose McKinley Wheeler. Deal?"

"No," Thomas replied with the return of his trademark smile. "I shall see you around seven thirty tomorrow morning, Jack."

Jack quickly looked up at Thomas and began, "that's too earl......"

"That will be just fine," said the lad, broadening his smile. "See you then."

Thomas returned to the cold night air as he walked out of Jack's front door and simultaneously placed the felt hat upon his head. As Thomas pulled out of Jack's drive, he just couldn't resist. The young man slowly turned the Chevrolet truck up river along the road. He hoped to get a look at the Club Palmetto from the road but was unsuccessful in doing so. The young man could not even see the road leading to the night club.

When Thomas wheeled back into the lot yard area of the Wheeler place, he noticed a light burning in the bunkhouse. The young man decided to go out to the bunkhouse and visit briefly with Amos. What Thomas found infuriated him.

Amos Washington set in his wooden rocker with a towel in his hand. With the towel, he gently dabbed blood from his battered face. His face was swollen and his eyes manifested pain and fear. This was not the Amos Washington that Thomas had grown up knowing. Amos however knew he was outmatched with Pierce's ruffians.

"How did it happen?" Thomas asked in a trembling voice.

"T'aint important," Amos replied. "It's been done an' that's that."

"Pierce do it?" Thomas demanded to know.

"I told you boy, it ain't important. Just forget it."

"Can't do that Amos," Thomas said. "How bad are you hurt?" He then asked.

"You see the most of it," Amos explained. "My sides ain't feelin' so well though. The pain is awful sharp boy."

After a few minutes of attempting to assist the old black gentleman, Thomas headed into town. It was in Live Oak he hoped to find the good Doctor Jones. Doc Jones was indeed a colorful character. He had practiced medicine in Suwannee County for many years. Doc had also drank and gambled in Suwannee County for many years. That particular night was no different. Doc Jones was in a low stakes poker game at Lefty's Tavern.

Thomas Wheeler suspected Doctor Jones would be at Lefty's because it was common talk of his love for gambling at the infamous beer joint. The young man knew Doc was inside Lefty's because his forty-one Chevrolet Deluxe Sedan was there. The car was solid black and Doc had bought it new. Thomas could easily identify it by the caved in fender. The good doctor had bent the car one week to the day after buying it.

As Thomas walked inside something occurred to him. For the first time ever, he had gone into a bar that night and was easily doing so for the second time in the same night. He did not care though. As far as he was concerned, Rose Wheeler could string him up by his heels. The only thing Thomas was concerned with was getting Amos medical attention.

Amos was like family to the Wheelers. Since Charles Wheeler had been away, Thomas had looked to the old black gentleman even more for guidance. He had been a friend, mentor, advocate, and even a disciplinarian to the young man.

There was a blue haze inside Lefty's. Apparently every patron inside the joint was smoking. Thomas found Lefty's to be much different than the other juke he had paid visit to earlier in the evening. The clientele did not appear as jovial nor did the man tending bar.

There was no live band but from a juke box came the sounds of sad music. Thomas had more of an appreciation for the jovial sounds he had heard earlier in the evening.

Lefty's was much larger in size and more people were there. There were only white folks in the joint and unlike the folks at The Club Palmetto, everyone stared at the lad. The Live Oak night club perhaps had nicer and more up to date furnishings but The Club Palmetto possessed a more sophisticated atmosphere and mood.

Thomas was directed by a young husky fellow to a side room. The entrance had no door but a white dingy curtain covered the opening. Inside the small room sat Doc Jones playing a hand of poker with three fellows Thomas thought to look like deadbeats.

"Doc Jones," Thomas called out with hat in hand.

"What's wrong boy?" The doctor asked in great concern.

"It's Amos Washington, Doc," Thomas began. "Some hoodlums beat the stew out of 'em."

"Where's he at?" The doctor asked without further looking at his hand.

"Out at our place," the young man answered. "Can you come, Doc?"

"I've got my bag in the car," Doc Jones replied. "Let's go."

As Thomas drove home, Doc Jones followed him. First and foremost Thomas was concerned about Amos. There was however another concern. The young man had to explain to his mother who had inflicted harm to their friend. Finally, Thomas knew what the assault would mean. Rose Wheeler was sure to mandate a move to Dead Man's Bay. Thomas however was determined not to give in. The young man certainly wished his father was home.

Naturally, Thomas was hoping to slip the doctor in and out without disturbing his mother. It wasn't so much that he was trying to hide the situation from her, he just didn't want her worrying. Unfortunately, his wish would not be granted.

As the two vehicles rolled to their complete stop between the Wheeler home and the bunk house, Rose came out.

"Thomas Wheeler, where have you been?" She demanded.

"Ma," he began, "there's been a little trouble and Amos needs the Doctor. Now everything is going to be O.K."

"Amos!" Rose yelled and placed her hands over her mouth. "Thomas what has happened?"

"He'll be O.K., Ma," Thomas assured his mother. "But we'll talk about it later."

Thomas Wheeler and his mother stood beside Amos Washington as Doctor Jones began listening to his heart beat.

Chapter VII

Around midnight, Doc Jones gave Thomas and Rose Wheeler a clear bill of health on their friend Amos. The verdict was a couple of broken ribs and a bruised body. No doubt, the doctor explained, Amos would be laid up for a few weeks. As for that night, rest would be important.

"He's tough as a mule," Doc said as he took a swig of remedy that was sold to him by a traveling medicine man.

Thomas was amused at the fact a genuine medical doctor might partake of a remedy sold by a traveling salesman that was merely a self proclaimed medicine man.

Amos soon dozed off and Doc Jones headed on out to return home. Thomas suggested to Rose that he sleep in the bunkhouse and see after Amos. Rose agreed but first demanded a conversation with her son inside.

"Yes ma'am," Thomas said forcing a smile as he sauntered toward the house.

Allen and Nancy were asleep inside so Rose was as quiet as she possibly could be under the circumstances.

"What on Earth happened tonight, Thomas Wheeler?" Rose demanded.

"I don't know everything Ma," Thomas calmly explained. "At this point all I know is that Scott Pierce and a couple of his goons beat up our Old Amos down there by the road."

"Well ain't this just a fine mess?" Rose commented. "Were you there?" she then asked.

"No ma'am," Thomas answered. "I was at the river."

The lad didn't really lie. He was at the river. Of course, he was not at the river for the reason Rose thought him to be.

"I think we need to take Amos and go to the Bay, Thomas," Rose said in an imperative tone. "I will not stay here and risk our lives because of a deadbeat criminal."

Thomas knew it was useless to argue with his mother at such an hour. Of course he knew it to be useless to argue at any hour.

"Why don't we get a nights rest and talk about it tomorrow, Ma," Thomas suggested.

"I don't want you leaving the place for a while," Rose replied. "There is no telling what that Pierce is capable of. I just wish I knew what he wants."

"He wan........," Thomas began. "I don't know what he wants but I do know this Ma. We've got a bunch of sweet potatoes to be dug and sold. We have that to do and you know it."

Rose Wheeler looked so concerned. She was indeed a strong woman but was beginning to wonder just how much more she could take. Furthermore, she knew what results contacting Sheriff Green would bring.

"Oh Thomas," she said. "it's not that I mean to be so hard on you. You are so good and work so hard. I just worry about you children. But you know what?" She asked her son with a smile.

"What's that Ma?" Thomas replied gently smiling back.

"One day soon your pa is going to come home and all will be better," Rose Wheeler said so confident.

Thomas certainly hoped she was correct and for a brief moment, he was also thinking just as positive. He could only think about the ones they had confirmed that would never return from war. Naturally he did not want to discuss that.

"Why don't I throw some wood on the fire, Ma?" Thomas suggested. "Tomorrow morning I am going to check with some fellows about hauling the potatoes to Jacksonville for us."

"O.K.," Rose said. "But first why don't you carry Allen and Nancy to school. Thank God they slept through this mess tonight."

"Yes ma'am," replied the young man.

Thomas was certainly glad Rose had eased up on his being grounded to the place. He was as free spirited as an eagle soaring above the flat woods. Besides, being grounded to the Wheeler farm would hinder his plans of Jack coming to their rescue.

Thomas was realizing he needed to obtain Jack's assistance for more than one reason. Sure he wanted Pierce deterred but he also wanted to see his mother's family somewhat reunited. Of course the lad was intelligent enough to realize such an aspiration to be nearly impossible.

Nonetheless the young Mr. Wheeler went to sleep that night with high hopes as he sat at the bedside of his friend and mentor Amos Washington. As he slept, pleasant dreams came. Thomas was accompanied by his father and uncles on a boat at Dead Man's Bay. They were catching speckled trout by the dozens where the Steinhachee River's mouth poured into the salty waters of the Gulf of Mexico.

Morning came soon enough and the crowing rooster disturbed Thomas' perfect fishing trip.

"Good mornin'," Amos said as Thomas began to rub his eyes.

"Good mornin'," the young man replied. "I'll make us some coffee."

"Your ma done an' brought it out here," Amos said through swollen lips, "an' breakfast too."

"How you feel?" Thomas asked sympathetically.

"Oh I's felt better. Course I's felt slightly worser too," the farm hand admitted while forcing a smile. "Me an' you needin' to talk Thomas."

"I'm listening," Thomas said as he ambled to the blue tin pot his mother had carried the coffee out in.

As the lad poured himself a cup of the hot brew, Amos started to speak.

"That fellow Pierce say he wants to see your pa," Amos began. "He didn't believe me when I told 'em Mr. Charles be gone in the war. I expect you knows why he ain't too awful fond of ya pa don't ya?"

"I know," Thomas said. "I know all about pa testifying in court to prosecute the no count, low dow........"

"All right boy," Amos interrupted, "watch what you say. Your ma gonna walk in on ya just as sure as the world."

Thomas smiled and offered his old buddy a cup of coffee. Upon Amos' acceptance, the young man poured two cups. He then handed Amos his and sat down with his own.

"What we gonna do 'bout that fellow Pierce?" Amos asked sincerely. "Your ma wants to run but we just can't do that Thomas. I ain't never ran in my life an' I wouldn't be too all fired proud to go an' start a runnin' now."

"What do you suggest?" Thomas probed.

Amos stared at the open beams over his head as he lay helpless in bed. For a moment he was silent but finally spoke. "Jack McKinley," he said. "Go and get 'em."

"I talked to Uncle Jack last night," Thomas replied.

Amos smiled temporarily but soon cringed as another sharp pain jolted throughout his torso. Relief was soon to follow and a subtle smile returned to his face. He and Thomas looked at one another in attempt to offer each other reassurance.

"What does Miss Rose think about your talkin' to your Uncle Jack?" Amos asked.

"Aw I don't know, Amos," the young man replied. "You know I don't think I mentioned to her I talked to Jack."

"Where did you see him at?" Amos then probed.

"Why do you ask?" Thomas quickly replied.

"Oh just wondering," the older gentleman replied with a slight smile. "I've heard through some of the other black folk around about somethin' called the Club Palmetto."

"You haven't been have you?" Thomas asked sincerely.

"No but I'm a aimin' to," Amos promised. "I sure 'nough a aimin' to go there."

Thomas stood and stretched his lanky torso as he looked outside the sole window in Amos' quarters. Outside he saw nothing but a typical crisp fall morning.

"You just get better Amos," Thomas began. "And I'll go and get Jack McKinley."

Inside the Wheeler home, Thomas held only brief conversation with his mother. Rose busied herself preparing to two younger Wheeler children for school. Rose had earlier advised Thomas against sharing with the two youngsters about Amos' misfortune. Thomas respected his mother's advice and told his younger siblings nothing of the previous night's events.

As Thomas began walking his brother and sister to the Chevrolet truck, Rose called out to him.

"Yea, Ma," Thomas replied as he sauntered back to the front porch of the one-story dwelling.

"Thomas," Rose began with a forced smile, "do be careful and come straight home as soon as you tend to your business in town."

"I will," Thomas assured with a smile.

After seeing Allen and Nancy into the school house, Thomas headed toward Jack McKinley's cabin. From Jack's chimney, smoke drifted without care and direction into the crisp autumn morning.

Just as Thomas figured, Jack was still sound asleep. He lay sprawled in front of the warm fireplace on a pallet of crocheted afghans. He remained in his trousers and at his feet were his displaced brogans, white shirt, and suspenders.

Without awaking his uncle, Thomas quietly drew enough water for a pot of coffee. He then found the grounds to boil a pot of coffee and as the water began boiling slightly, Thomas woke Jack.

"Wake up, Jack," the lad called.

As Jack removed the green afghan that only partially covered his torso, Thomas saw the forty-five caliber handgun. Without sound, Jack stood and slowly looked outside.

"What time is it?" Jack finally asked.

"Eight thirty," Thomas replied. "Sorry I'm late but I had to carry Allen and Nancy to school this morning."

"You're not late you are early," Jack hastily said.

Thomas didn't reply, he just smiled at Jack.

After Jack slowly got ready for the day, he sat down to a cup of coffee with Thomas. Over coffee, Thomas filled his uncle in on the events of the prior night involving poor Amos. Jack made no comment. He quietly listened as Thomas carefully gave account of the whole unfortunate ordeal.

Finally Jack was ready. As the two men walked outside the cabin's door, Jack grabbed his rifle that was usually propped just inside the door against the dingy wall.

"You want to take my coupe?" Jack asked Thomas.

"No," the lad replied, "I'm gonna pick up a few things in town."

The two boarded the Chevrolet truck and Jack lit a Lucky Strike cigarette. Thomas watched a couple of squirrels play carelessly until they scampered up a Laurel Oak. He then studied his uncle for a moment.

"What are you waiting for kid?" Jack asked.

"We ought to go and talk to Ma," Thomas began.

"About what?" Questioned Jack. "I wouldn't think she'd be so keen on talking to me about Pierce or anything else for that matter."

"I just think it would be the right thing to do," Thomas admitted.

Jack looked at his nephew for a moment and took a few deep draws from his cigarette. Thomas on the other hand just looked forward into the river woods behind Jack's cabin.

"You came to me for help, Thomas, and I am prepared to do that. But you didn't say anything about getting Rose's approval," Jack explained.

"It's up to you," Thomas said. "No hard feelings either way."

"Let's go," Jack conceded.

So they were off. The young Mr. Wheeler drove the Chevrolet truck back to the Wheeler residence. As Thomas turned off the dirt road and headed up toward the house, he detected a look of reminiscence in Jack. The lad's uncle appeared to be recalling his childhood days. As Jack glared about the pecan trees, Thomas saw the slight grin upon his face. The young man had to wonder if Jack too, had at one time strongly disliked the chore of picking up pecans.

Jack then looked at the McKinley home which had been known for sometime as the Wheeler home and smiled.

"The old house looks good," Jack said. "Ya'll have really taken care of it. The whole place looks good, Thomas."

"Pa always worked hard around here. Since he's been gone Ma's been crackin' the whip on Ole Amos and me," Thomas explained.

"I would like to see Amos," Jack advised. "It's been a while."

"O.K.. But first we have to see her," Thomas said while pointing toward his mother.

Rose stood at the clothes line hanging a few clothes out to dry. She looked at the truck coming up the drive in curiosity of Thomas' early return. Upon seeing a passenger, she immediately ceased her duties and began walking toward the barn where her son was soon to park.

As Thomas and Jack got out of the truck, Rose stood without speaking. Her arms were crossed and a look of concern was in her eyes.

"Well look what the cats drug up," Rose slowly said in a soft tone.

"Hello, Rose," Jack then said. "It's been a while."

Thomas stood a few feet away smiling. He was so proud of himself having reunited his mother and her brother.

"Yes it has," she replied with a gentle smile.

"How have you been Rose?" Jack asked.

"Well O.K. I suppose considering everything," said Rose. "But don't you think maybe you should have asked long before now big brother?"

Jack looked down as he shuffled his right foot about in the sand. He then looked up at his sister a bit sheepishly. Thomas on the other hand was beginning to feel nervous about the way this conversation was beginning to shape up.

"Rose," Jack began, "don't you know that road goes both ways. You know my life hasn't been all that pleasant the past few years either."

"Thomas go inside," Rose demanded.

"But Ma," Thomas retorted.

"Don't you but Ma me, Thomas Wheeler," Rose exclaimed in a very stern voice. "I told you to go into the house and that is well what I mean. Now get."

Much to Jack and Rose's surprise, the young gentleman offered a moderate smile and without further argument somewhat obeyed his mother's demand. He did not go inside the Wheeler home but he did saunter out to Amos' quarters.

"Jack McKinley's out there," Thomas told Amos as the young man peered out the window at his mother and uncle in conversation.

Amos smiled softly and remained quiet. Perhaps there was nothing to say. Maybe he just didn't want to ruin a perfectly good moment of reminiscence with conversation. Nonetheless, Amos continued to smile as only he could.

Meanwhile, Jack and Rose continued their conversation outside. Thomas smiled gently as he assumed their conversation would lighten and once again the McKinley family may work together. He did realize it would not be easily accomplished but then again he also knew he was Thomas Wheeler.

"That is some boy," Jack said of Thomas to Rose.

"Ain't he though?" Rose replied with a warming tone in her voice. "I don't know what I would do without him. But sometimes he's just so head strong, Jack, I don't know what to do."

"So he takes after his mother, does he?" Jack asked with a smile.

Expressionless, Rose responded, "Actually he is a cross between his Uncle Jack and Uncle Warren."

Jack suddenly looked at Rose as if she had slapped him. His blue eyes were focused only by fury. His square jaw was dropped just a bit and slowly he allowed his head to rock back and then down never losing eye contact with Rose.

"Warren McKinley," Jack said in resentment, "now that is a soul I haven't seen in years. In fact I stay clear of the Bay just because I don't want to see the bum."

"And he doesn't come to Suwannee County just to avoid you," Rose retorted.

"How are Mama and Papa doing, Rose?" Jack then asked.

"They have let the past go, Jack," Rose said. "Maybe we should."

"Maybe so," Jack agreed. "Let's see how things go with Pierce first."

Rose then smiled at her brother. It was a smile of acceptance and forgiveness. Inside, Amos and Thomas also smiled. They knew Pierce would soon be answering to the legendary Jack McKinley.

Chapter VIII

Rose Wheeler prepared quite a meal that day for lunch. She had baked sweet potatoes to go with the pork tender loins, grits, and biscuits. To further embellish an already perfect meal, strawberry preserves were also placed on the table.

Jack McKinley did not even attempt to engage in conversation as he steadily ate. Thomas watched in amazement as his uncle consumed more food than the lad had ever seen any one man consume. As the young man looked at his mother in disbelief, she gave him a wink and smiled.

"Well," Thomas finally began, "when you get finished what do you say we ride into town Uncle Jack?"

"What's the rush?" Jack replied as he readied himself to devour another biscuit. "Pierce isn't going to try anything today."

"How do we know that?" The boy asked.

"Because he went to the river," Jack answered. "I watched him and two brutes load up that fancy car while your ma was cooking this fine meal and you were discussing your potato digging with Amos. I brought my binoculars. They carried life vests and fishing gear."

"How do you know they went to the river?" The boy probed.

"I happen to know our friend Mr. Pierce keeps a sizable boat down near Branford. They tell me he runs the thing all the way to the mouth of the river," Jack explained. "After while we'll ride into town and check into what Pierce has been up to. The more we know about him the less he can do with us."

"Sounds good," Thomas replied with his trademark smile.

"Always know your enemy, Thomas," Jack said as he began helping Rose clear the table.

Thomas joined in as usual and began washing dishes. Upon completion, Rose walked to the front porch and sat down in a rocking chair. There, she would await J.G. Phillips in hopes of mail from her beloved husband Charles Wheeler. Once again J.G. would bring no news from Charles.

Thomas enjoyed a visit with Amos while Jack slowly walked about the yards of his own boyhood home. Jack found the place to be more modern and refreshing. Although he had many pleasant memories there, he was pleased to see the necessary changes made.

After a while, Jack and Thomas set out for Live Oak in the Chevrolet truck. As the two slowly traveled the sand bed roads, Jack quietly reminisced his past.

"Are you as bad to drink as folks say?" Thomas asked bluntly.

Undoubtedly Jack was caught by total surprise. He did however answer with tact and without hostility.

"Well," he replied, "I suppose that depends upon how badly these folks claim I drink. I for one think I am a pretty good drinker. Maybe the best."

Thomas laughed irrepressibly at his uncle's wit. No more was said about Jack's alleged problem. Both Thomas and Jack turned their attention to the situation at hand. No matter how good Jack McKinley might be or rather might have once been, a game plan was necessary when squaring off with Scott Pierce.

"I do have to check with a couple of fellows in town about hauling some sweet potatoes. That is what I was supposed to be doing when I picked you up this morning," Thomas advised his uncle.

"That will be fine," Jack replied. "While you work on that I will nose around town and find out what Pierce is up to. What do you say we meet up at Mason's about four?"

"You've got it," Thomas said as he continued to drive into town.

When the uncle-nephew team reached Live Oak, Thomas parked in front of Mason's and the two went their separate ways. Just as Thomas figured, he saw Bradley Matthews unloading fruit at Conner's Produce Stand. He swiftly walked across the street and bargained with Mr. Matthews to transport the potatoes to the Jacksonville market some time in the weeks to come.

The young man then meandered down the street and found Archibald Miller parked in front of his brother Chester's gas station. Archibald was a nervous character. He wore khaki shirts and khaki pants. Although he stood just under six feet tall, Archibald appeared much taller due to his extremely thin frame. His hair was awful thin and graying and appeared to be glued down to his head.

Early in life, Archibald Miller's nose had been broken by a kicking milk cow and due to the times, the nose had grown crooked. Every time Thomas saw Archibald the nervous man would ask such questions as does my hair look straight or do my pants fit me.

Normally, Thomas would avoid Mr. Archibald Miller but that particular day he would just have to deal with the strange questions. The man was terribly self conscious.

"You still hauling vegetables to Tampa?" Thomas asked.

"Occasionally," Miller replied. "Why have you heard someone complaining? Why I will ta......,"

"No no," Thomas hastily replied. "Nothing like that. I just wanted to employ your services to haul some potatoes down there for me."

Thomas Wheeler and Archibald Miller struck up a deal for the Wheeler's potatoes to be transported to the Tampa market. In just that short time, Thomas had organized the distribution of their fall crop.

Upon bidding Archibald and his brother Chester a farewell, Thomas journeyed toward Mason's to meet up with Jack. Of course Jack wasn't at Mason's when Thomas got there but Thomas enjoyed casual conversation with Mr. Mason.

One hour later, Thomas began looking at the clock upon the wall hoping for Jack to soon return. Finally the lad looked at the Mason's, smiled and tipped his hat. When he walked onto the street, he knew exactly where good old Uncle Jack was. Jack was at Lefty's Bar. Lefty's sat caddy cornered across from the barber shop. From the bar, Thomas heard loud voices and then a sudden quiet overtook the place. The young man watched several patrons abruptly evacuate the place.

Just as quickly, Thomas made his way over and inside the tavern to possibly rescue his uncle. Just as Thomas figured, Jack was squared off with a craggy looking character.

"Jack McKinley," the other man said in a shaking voice. "You worked me over in thirty-eight and now I'm a gonna set things straight."

Jack smiled and rolled up his sleeves as the two circled one another eye to eye. They looked just like two roosters about to engage in battle.

"Not today gentlemen," Thomas said. "Now I can't drink but if'n you two buzzards will just settle down, drinks are on me."

"Go on kid," Jack's opponent said.

"Uncle Jack," Thomas softly said. "Please don't, me and Ma need you too bad right now." Thomas looked at the other man and said, "Mr., I'll pay you not to fight him."

No more had to be said. The two quarrelsome men had just enough grace left about them they could actually hear a young man's cry for help. Therefore, a fight went without being fought.

"You're drunk Uncle Jack," Thomas said in disapproval.

"What if I am?" Jack retorted. "When the day comes a man can't stop off and have himself a drin...."

"Forget it," Thomas responded in extreme disgust. "Maybe you should just stay here and drink. I'll handle the situation at home my own self. I don't think you particularly wanted to help anyway. I'm sorry I bothered you."

The lad then turned and briskly began walking out of the bar. Jack McKinley looked at the wooden floor as Thomas paced out. Mixed emotions stormed McKinley's heart and soul. To begin with, he had never been stood up to like that before. Furthermore, he felt like a lowlife. Jack McKinley had realized in a short time his nephew was an extremely proud young man. He also realized it was probably not easy for Thomas to ask for help. More than likely the young man had never before asked anyone for such help as he had asked Jack.

"Hold on," Jack said softly. "I can do better for you Thomas. Give me another shot will you."

Thomas stopped and looked at his uncle without sporting his trademark smile. "I only want your help if you want to help," Thomas said. "It's up to you Jack."

Together the two walked out of Lefty's and marched to the Chevrolet truck. From there they would ride back to the Wheeler home.

Jack McKinley was borderline drunk and Thomas Wheeler was totally mad. The young man wanted so to say something but only knew he would bolt out uncontrollably if he did speak. Therefore he maintained silence while driving the Chevrolet harder than ever before. Of course Jack detected his nephew's anger but chose to be quiet as well.

The newly formed uncle-nephew team was only a couple of miles from the Wheeler place when Jack broke the silence. "We have to get your ma and the kids to go down to the bay for a few days, Thomas," he said.

Thomas acted as if though he had not heard his uncle. He continued to drive fiercely home. A couple of miles later, Thomas pulled the truck off the grade and shut it off.

"What are you doing?" Jack asked.

"I want to know why you think Ma and the kids need to go to the Bay," Thomas demanded.

"You want to know?" Jack answered intensely. "I'll tell you why. I found out back there at Lefty's that our little friend Scott Pierce is planning to have a lot of fun makin' your ma's life miserable."

"Who told you that?" Thomas asked in a softer tone.

"Bob Martin," Jack replied. "Bob tends bar for Lefty nowadays. He knows I'm your ma's brother. You see, Thomas, Scott Pierce evidently goes into Lefty's a whole bunch. According to Bob the man is crazy, I mean plumb deranged."

Jack then paused and said no more as Thomas looked straight out into the woods. The young man had such a tortured look about him but somehow managed to regain a slight smile.

"Bob Martin must have said something else," Thomas suggested.

"He is so deranged according to Bob that he thinks your pa is hid-ing from him in your house. Thomas, he plans on burning him out."

"I wouldn't think Pierce would just go into Lefty's and tell that sort of stuff," the boy commented.

"Of course not," Jack said, "he's been discussing it with his goons. They go in, get drunk, and forget Bob is listening in. I can't take a fellow that can't handle his booze," Jack added.

Thomas didn't comment for a few minutes he just sat in the truck and gazed out the window. Finally he removed his hat slightly and repositioned it further back on his head. At last Jack felt as if he were making leeway with his nephew.

"You gonna mention to Ma about her and the kids goin' down there?" Thomas asked.

"I need you to be with me on this," Jack said.

"I'm with you," the boy replied with an ever so slight smile.

"That ain't all I'll be needin'," Jack then mentioned.

"Oh yea," Thomas replied with a touch of surprise in his voice, "what else are you going to be needin' Jack?"

"I want you to go to the bay with them Thomas," Jack said carefully. "It's not that I don't want you ar....."

"Forget it," Thomas interrupted.

Jack and Thomas sat in silence as they each stared in different directions. It wasn't that Jack did not want his nephew around, he just didn't want to see the boy hurt. Jack McKinley was not naive altogether when trouble of this sort was brewing. He was also smart enough to know he would be unable to change his nephew's feelings at the present.

Thomas snorted in discontent. "You know Jack," he began, "for over four years now I've had to be a man when I wanted to be a boy. There was times I wanted so bad to play like other kids when there was man's work to be done. I was the one that had to do it and never one time complained. In all those years I never saw you trying to help or protect me. Now I ask for your help and you want to tell me I am in the way."

Nothing else was said. Thomas Wheeler cranked up the Chevrolet truck and journeyed toward Jack's cabin. When they made it to the cabin, Thomas remained quiet.

"I guess this is where I get out," Jack said.

"Reckon so," the boy replied. "See you around."

As Jack stood behind his Ford coupe, he watched his nephew drive away. He knew Thomas was a hard kid. He also knew the boy was capable of handling the upcoming trouble as any grown man around. Most of all, Jack realized what the potential loss of Thomas would do to Rose. With her husband gone, Jack knew she didn't need the boy gone too.

Chapter IX

After dropping Jack off at his cabin, Thomas headed home. However, he changed his mind and rode down to Charles Springs. Thomas often looked to the spring for solitude. It was not far from his home and he truly believed God had added an extra touch of tranquillity to that special place.

Thomas also realized the unique past in the spring. Not far down river nearly a half a century earlier, a locomotive had plunged into the churning waters of the Suwannee River. Nearly one century earlier, Mrs. Rebecca Charles had lost her life at the hands of hostile Indians while approaching the spring.

Indeed Thomas knew Charles Springs had listened to many problems and felt his could maybe be shared with this ever trusting pool of water. For a while, the young man skipped rocks. Next, he watched the fishes swimming in such harmony about the crystal clear water as he wondered why humans could not be as such. Finally the lad lay upon a rock and watched the dove beautify the skies with their harmonic flight.

Time went by so quickly as Thomas Wheeler lay at peace with such a tranquil environment. The river woods were so undisturbed and unconquered. Virgin timber stood about the Water Oaks. The ground was accented by Palmetto while Spanish Moss hung insouciantly from the oaks.

Thomas thought about his situation at hand very carefully. Deep down he knew Jack McKinley was right but it was not his nature to admit it. Another little thing called pride was to prevent the lad from returning to his uncle. He did know it was inevitable that he speak with his mother concerning a stay at Dead Man's Bay.

"Your ma said I could find you here," Amos said.

"Amos!" The young man exclaimed as he sprung from the rock. "What on earth are you doing out? You know what Doc Jones said."

"We were all getting worried about you, Thomas Wheeler," Amos commented authoritatively. "Jack came by 'bout an hour ago and said you'd left his cabin a couple of hours before that."

"Who needs Jack McKinley?" Thomas asked sarcastically.

"We all do," Amos replied with his gentle smile. "He tells us what Pierce has on his mind. Thomas I don't think me and you gonna be able to fight them hoodlums off by ourselves. Why don't me an' you go on down to the bay with your ma an' the kids an' leave the feudin' up to Jack. Lawd know he sure good in the feudin' business."

Thomas Wheeler felt so betrayed. Of course he had not been, but how was a young man of fourteen to feel. He had worked as any grown man for the past several years. Furthermore, he was known to think with a steady head. At last, his steady head would appear to prevail.

"O.K.," Thomas conceded with an ever so slight smile. "I'll go for you, Amos, if you say that's best. But I won't like it."

Amos smiled approvingly. "I know you won't," he admitted, "but that is the best thing to do Thomas."

Thomas slowly stood and began to walk to the truck when suddenly he became puzzled. "How did you get here Amos?" The lad asked.

"Jack dropped me off on his way back to the cabin," Amos answered.

"Ya'll were that sure of where I was?" Thomas then asked in amazement.

As Amos smiled and walked in substantial pain, he looked at Thomas. "Thomas Wheeler," he began, "don't go through this life a thinkin' that ma of your's don't always know what you be doin' because she does."

In a short while, Thomas and Amos had returned to the Wheeler home. Amos would go directly to his own quarters and begin packing what items he would need for the Bay. He had been there many times before while employed with the McKinley and Wheeler families. Each time there he had served a purpose and sought to do no different this particular trip. Although he predominately prided himself an excellent farmhand, he was no slouch in a fish camp either.

Inside the Wheeler home, Thomas found his mother quickly packing only the items she and the younger children would need. As for Thomas, he was to do his own packing.

"We goin' to see Granny an' Pappa McKinley," Nancy happily announced to her older brother, Thomas.

In an earnest attempt to act just as enthused, Thomas smiled at his little sister. He then picked her up over his head and said, "We sure are Nancy and I'm gonna eat all the shrimp I can hold. How about you?"

"Not me," Nancy said. "I'm going to eat crab claws and so is Allen."

"Well O.K. then," Thomas replied, "go on and get everything you'll need at the Bay."

As Nancy went about her innocent business, Thomas poured himself a piece of a cup of coffee. He searched for the right words but was unable to come up with anything of comfort for his mother.

"I'm sorry, Ma," he began, "you know I just let the time get away from me again."

"You got it honest son," Rose replied calmly. "Your pa is the world's worst about doing that very thing."

Rose Wheeler then smiled at her son and sat down at the kitchen table. She was beginning to possess such a wearisome look.

"I know," Thomas said with a slight grin.

"That's why I know he's O.K. Thomas. You do think he is O.K. too, don't you Thomas?" Rose asked in search of Thomas's voice of assurance.

"He'll be just fine, Ma," Thomas said in such an assuring manner. "Old J.G. Phillips should bring us a letter from Pa any day now."

"We won't have to be at the bay too long," Rose commented. "I appreciate your understanding son," she then said.

"No problem," Thomas replied. "We need a few days of salty air anyhow."

"Jack will be staying here while we're away. He's going to take care of all the feeding up and even talked like he may be able to see to getting the potatoes dug too. We'll drive his coupe and he'll keep the truck here," Rose instructed. "That's O.K. with you isn't it."

"Sure, Ma," Thomas said forcing a smile as he walked outside.

The young man walked about the barn area. If only his father were here, he thought. He wasn't though and Jack would be in charge. Thomas could not understand why he was now being considered too young for a man's job. The lad was, however man enough to know his mother did not need any additional stress placed on her shoulders so he had chosen not to push the issue.

Since the young man was such good friends with the few farm animals the Wheelers had, he went out to bid each of them a farewell.

"Now you do right while I'm away," he told each of them individually. "I'll be back before you even know I'm gone."

Thomas then journeyed into Amos' quarters. The gentleman was packing a few belongings to carry along. The last item Amos had laid out to pack was his worn Bible. The gent saw Thomas looking at the Bible.

"It looks all wore out don't it?" Amos asked rhetorically with his kind smile. "The good word don't never wear out though."

"Amos," Thomas began, "we need to buy you a new Bible."

"Why?" Amos replied. "This one does just fine. It's the only thing I have to remember my folks by. You know Thomas, this here Bible belonged to my grandparents. They were slaves you know. Now it belongs to me. It's the only thing I have that was theirs. My granpappy, he could read. I reckoned he was the first of my people to learn how an' he'd read this Bible to us a whole bunch when I was a little boy."

"Is that right?" Thomas asked as Amos lit his pipe.

"That's a fact," Thomas said. "But it's all I need. You see, they gave me strength by givin' me this here Bible. I find in tough times like this, I can read it and the Good Lord will tell me what I be needin' to do."

"I never knew you had a streak of religion," Thomas commented.

"Well I do," Amos said. "I know you goin' through some struggles right now, Thomas, and I suggest you look in your own good book."

Thomas smiled broadly. "I don't think you could be more right," he agreed. "I reckon we'll be leaving out in the morning. If you need me to help you get ready in any way just let me know."

Upon leaving Amos in his quarters, Thomas slowly walked about the yard. The oak and pecan trees gave much character to the Wheeler place. Although nothing was fancy about the place, a certain tone of home would overshadow it for generations of the McKinley Family. Thomas was the third generation.

On the front porch, Thomas found Allen and Nancy playing school. Behind the Crepe Myrtle Bush, Thomas stood and watched. It was a joy for him to find at least two content beings. Allen was playing the role of a strict teacher and chronically refused to allow his unworthy pupil to speak. Even the old cat was scared to get up and walk.

Thomas' moment of peace was interrupted by the sound of J.G. Phillips' car making it's way down the grade to deliver the mail. As J.G. rolled to a stop, Thomas was awaiting him at the mailbox.

"Hello, Thomas," J.G. said.

"J.G.," Thomas replied, "got me any good news?"

"Got a letter from you Grandma McKinley," responded the mailman. "I'm sorry I don't have anything from Charles."

"Ain't your fault," Thomas admitted with a sad smile. "Me and Ma and the kids are gonna be down at the Bay for a few days J.G.. If by chance you do get a hold to some good news,.........."

"I'll bring it all the way there to you, Thomas," J.G. Phillips assured.

"You're the best, J.G.," said Thomas, "and I appreciate it, too."

J.G. Phillips was gone and Thomas Wheeler stood alone in front of his home. He had in his own way come to terms with leaving Suwannee County for a few days. He did however secretly vow to never again be driven away by the likes of Scott Pierce. The young man made the promise and would have to live with it from there out.

Night soon fell and Thomas Wheeler remained inside his home feeling little different than a prisoner. He peered outside through his bedroom window and across the way, he could see no evidence of life at Pierce's place. Undoubtedly, the swindler without personality had failed thus far to return.

For approximately twenty minutes the young man peered through the window as Allen hopelessly attempted to draw a picture of their missing father and Nancy played quietly with a doll. Meanwhile Rose cleaned up the kitchen in conclusion of their last day at home for a while.

At last, Thomas saw the light of a vehicle coming down the road. He was curious as to who it could be. His only logical choice would be Pierce. Quietly he stepped over to his dresser and carefully took out a forty-five caliber revolver.

The lad then rushed back to the window and just as he had anticipated, the car was pulling off the main road and up the Wheeler drive. Cautiously, he opened his window in hopes his mother and siblings would not hear and waited for the intruder to make his presence. Thomas Wheeler fully intended to shoot.

The moon and stars offered little light for Thomas to see his possible target. Once the car stopped he tried hard to focus. He was sure of only one thing, the automobile was of a very dark color. Finally, Thomas heard the automobile's motor turn off. The silence was soon followed by the slamming of two doors. Faster and faster his heart pounded as he inadequately tried to target in on his foe.

At last, he heard voices. They were familiar voices. It was the voices of some old friends of his parents. Wilbur and Estelle Porter would occasionally stop by unannounced for an overnight stay. That again was apparently the case.

Thomas Wheeler did not care much for the Porters but tolerated them for two reasons. First out of respect of his parents and secondly, he was too young to oppose his parents friends.

Wilbur and Estelle Porter never had children of their own but somehow deemed themselves authorities on child raising. The young Mr. Wheeler found that to be rather irritating. Whether or not there was any truth to it, Thomas wholeheartedly felt he suffered the consequences of each of their visits for a minimum of two weeks to follow.

Undoubtedly he would hear Mrs. Porter remind his mother of the benefits of administering caster oil to growing boys. She often explained how caster oil was the cure all for flues, ring worms, tape worms, colds, and general male adolescence. In all actuality Estelle Porter was a very pretty lady. She appeared to be very delicate and always presented herself in an elegant fashion with a strong hint of silver hair. It was her domineering manner however that so displeased Thomas.

Wilbur on the other hand did not appear to be as assertive with his own hair brain ideas. He was perhaps a bit more subtle and Thomas was not fooled by his front in the least. Mr. Porter was notorious for planting senseless ideas into Charles Wheeler's head for Thomas to do. Porter fancied himself as a scientist. He would share his ideas with Charles about having Thomas infiltrate the ground in one foot increments with a dabble to aerate the ground around pecan trees. Another of Porter's ideas was to have Thomas separate six shoats and put them in individual pens. From there, he would feed them various combinations of feed and chart their growth rates as well as feed costs.

Quietly, Thomas listened to his mother welcome these two annoying persons with open arms. The only good thing he could think about his father's situation was that Wilbur Porter could not plant any ideas into Charles Wheeler's head. That part was almost comforting.

Wilbur and Estelle Porter were distant relatives of the McKinley family. They lived in Valdosta, Georgia and would usually come through once every three or four months. Wilbur was a graduate of the University of Florida's School of Horticulture. While attending college at Florida, he made a life long friend with another Florida graduate from High Springs, Florida. Over the years Wilbur and Estelle had visited back and forth with his old college chum and his wife. Each time they were returning to Valdosta, the Porters would stop in on the Wheelers and ruin Thomas' life for a short while.

Although Thomas did not want to, he knew it was in his best interest to make a friendly appearance at that moment. He would greet his adversaries with a smile and allow Mrs. Porter to pinch his cheeks while Wilbur would go on about what a fine man Thomas was going to make. How disgusting, the lad thought to himself.

Finally Thomas appeared in the living room. Things were just as he had anticipated. Estelle had already began sharing helpful hints with Rose while Wilbur gave Allen and Nancy each a penny. When they saw Thomas, he wasn't really treated much different than his younger siblings.

The Porters declined all the food offered by Rose Wheeler. They did however willingly accept a cup of coffee. Once again, they were making themselves quite at home. At last, Thomas came up with a break free line.

"I must feed up," the young man advised.

"I thought that was already done," Rose quickly responded.

"Well," the young man muttered, "I didn't get finished so I reckon I'll be finishing up now."

"Well now," Wilbur Porter said, "why don't I come out and give you a hand Sonny."

Thomas thought silently. My name ain't Sonny and I don't need your help. He did as all good boys should do though and remained polite. "No, thank you," he replied, "it won't take but a minute."

"I see," Porter said with a slight smile, "I need to speak with you concerning an important matter if you will."

"Well come on then," replied the young man as he began a subtle saunter out the kitchen door. He did somehow force his trademark smile as well.

Inside the corn crib, Thomas scooped up a pail full of cracked corn and carried it out to the hog pin. Porter watched carefully to insure the young man conducted his chore in the proper manner.

After dumping the feed into the oblong wooden trough, Thomas looked sincerely at Mr. Porter. "What is on you mind, sir?" The lad asked bluntly.

"We came through town a few days ago and saw you in Live Oak with Jack," Porter said.

"That stands to reason," Thomas replied as he hung the pail upon a nail on a board outside the hog pin. "He's been helping out around here some. In fact, he's gonna watch the place while we're down at the Bay for a few days."

"I see," Porter said with a sarcastic grin.

"Why do you ask?" Thomas asked just as sardonic.

"Well," Porter sheepishly began, "everyone knows Jack has had some problems. I just don't think he could be such a great influence on you."

"You need not worry about influences on me, Mr. Porter," the young man explained. "I ain't stupid but I ain't worldly either," he added while walking away.

"I saw Warren yesterday," Porter then said.

Thomas turned back to Porter and asked, "Where did you see my Uncle Warren?"

"Mouth of the Suwannee," Porter replied with his derisive grin. "My old college buddy and I took an afternoon ride to the coast and there Old Warren was there just as big as you please."

"Talk to 'em?" Thomas asked.

"Oh no," Porter answered. "He was on another fellow's boat. Your Uncle Warren looked like he was talking about something awful serious with this other fellow so I didn't bother him."

"Is that a fact?" The young man nonchalantly replied.

"That's a fact," Porter said. "That other fellow was this here Scott Pierce that got your grandparents old place."

Thomas stopped and turned to face Porter. Porter did not see the uneasy look of a boy but that of a young man for the first time.

Chapter X

The beautiful sound of a harmonic voice sifted outward from inside the four walls of The Club Palmetto. The lady sang so gracefully as the lazy piano provided elegant background music to accompany her lovely words. It was truly a peaceful song in a peaceful atmosphere.

As Jack McKinley walked inside the club, Zeb shuffled on back to the table at which Jack customarily sat.

"How's about it Jack?" The tall lean black gentleman asked as the two men sat down.

Jack just looked at Zeb with half a smile and lit a Lucky Strike. He handed the cigarette to Zeb and then lit another for himself. After inhaling deeply, Jack McKinley slowly exhaled.

"Who's the duo performing there?" Jack inquired.

"That, my friend, is probably the best of their kind anywhere," Zeb proudly announced. "The lady is Virdie Hollister and her accomplice there on the ivories is a man friend of hers. His name just happens to be Lewis Whitley. I know you done heard of him now ain't you?"

"Can't say as I have," Jack replied with an increasing smile.

"I thought everbody done heard of him," Zeb candidly admitted. "You for sure you ain't?"

"New York, Orleans, Chicago?" Jack probed to learn of the talented musician's origin.

"Jacksonville," Zeb answered with a slight smile of his own.

Jack then got up and walked over to and around behind the bar. He removed a quart of sparkling moonshine and opened it as he walked over to the table where Zeb remained.

Whitley had begun playing his own rendition of My Old Dixie Flame on the piano and Ms. Hollister was resting her lovely voice. A few couples sashayed across the tiny dance area as Jack intensely drank the shine.

"Where you been gettin' off to lately?" Zeb asked.

After a moment of silence, Jack was ready to talk.

"Zeb," he began, "you know you are probably my best friend."

No doubt about it, Jack was telling his old friend the truth. They probably were best friends and their friendship had gone back many years. It had been a friendship originated on owing one another favors.

Some years prior while driving some of the fine cattle the McKinley Family had once owned, Jack had ridden up on Zeb attached to the end of a rope. It was near the Suwannee River where Zeb had crossed into Suwannee County from Madison County. While riding across on the ferry, the then younger black gent was playing Yankee Doodle Dandee on his horn. Some sons of the confederacy who were nearby fishing obviously did not approve so they began taking matters into their own hands. The confident Zeb commenced to stand up to them so they decided to put an end to the troublemaker once and for all.

That was where Jack McKinley came in. He just happened to ride up and observed the men getting ready to allow the black stranger to plummet to death off a horse's back. With the grace of a riverboat gambler and the austerity of a hungry miner, Jack McKinley pulled his gun and simply demanded, "cut him down!"

It was just another episode of the Jack McKinley saga. The men wanted to know who he was, he told them, and they cut his new found friend down. Jack McKinley had no intent of becoming such good friends with Zeb at that moment. Zeb was however just as mind strong as McKinley was. He vowed not to leave the Suwannee Valley area until he could repay the favor of the white stranger.

Although Zeb never found the opportunity to repay Jack in such a manner Zeb might have found sufficient, he had been a very good friend to Jack through the years. There had been endless fishing excursions, difficult jobs, cattle drives, and such. Indeed the two had became close friends over the years.

When the two first met on that fateful afternoon on the Suwannee River, Zeb was passing through on his way to Tampa. Since he needed to make a little traveling money at the time and Jack needed a cow hand, the two teamed up for what later appeared to be for life.

The years had brought Zeb and Jack to the Club Palmetto. Ironically, the years had been kinder to Zeb than to Jack. Together they were drinking that jar of moonshine as Jack continued speaking to Zeb.

"Zeb," he began, "my sister's boy needs me to help them out for a while."

"Seems like a nice boy," Zeb commented.

"He is a headstrong little fellow," Jack replied with a smile. "So full of life and hope. But you know, he's about as headstrong as his mama."

"Well," Zeb began with a serious look about him, "I ain't seen nobody with McKinley blood in 'em yet that ain't headstrong. But don't worry about things around here. I'll take care of everything while your busy with your folks."

Things continued at a mellow pace in the Club Palmetto for another thirty minutes or so. Jack was conversing with one of the couples who had been enjoying the talents of Miss Virdie and Lewis when Thomas Wheeler entered the building as if he were a regular guest of Club Palmetto.

Jack noticed off hand his nephew was not smiling. The boy stood straight and walked directly to Jack. The otherwise observant Thomas did not care to overlook his surroundings that particular evening. It was quite obvious he was there for one reason only.

The polite young man stood at a distance of a few feet as Jack wrapped up insignificant conversation with the couple. Upon Jack turning his attention to Thomas, the uncle pointed toward the front door and the two meandered over to Jack's cabin.

As Jack was brewing fresh coffee, Thomas began explaining to him of the Porters' visit. "You know," he started, "I know it isn't proper for me to be saying this, but they get on my nerves, Jack."

Jack calmly smiled and replied, "I thought I was the only person in the McKinley Family they bothered. It seems like they talk about everything except what's really their own business."

"Well this time good Ole' Mr. Porter had some information I found to be rather interesting," Thomas commented.

"And what was that?" Jack asked.

For a moment Thomas stared at the coffee pot. He mulled over what he was about to tell his uncle. The young man's eyes focused sternly upon the metal pot.

"Thomas," Jack called out, "I don't have all night. Now if you have something to tell me then tell me."

"Warren was talking to Pierce down at the mouth of the river," the young man finally said sadistically.

Needless to say, such news infuriated Jack. His own brother talking with the enemy. In fact it was his own brother talking with the enemy that had gotten their sister's family in this mess to begin with. Jack did not say anything for some time however. He poured himself and his nephew a cup of coffee each. They then quietly sat down at the small kitchen table and remained in silence for a short while longer.

"It doesn't surprise me," Jack softly commented. "It doesn't feel none to good, but it doesn't surprise me."

"I'm sorry Jack," Thomas said.

"It isn't your fault," Jack responded without expression. "How did Porter find out?"

"He was down there yesterday and saw them," the young man explained. "I figured maybe I should tell you."

"I wonder what kind of deal those two have plotted?" Jack asked.

"I don't know," Thomas admitted. "But I'll tell you this much, I don't think we need to be going to the bay if Warren's chummy with the enemy."

"To the contrary," Jack admitted. "I have a crafty plan of my own."

The young Mr. Wheeler smiled with much pride. He knew deep down that having Jack and Amos on his side, winning the Pierce war would be a sure bet.

"What's the plan?" Thomas anxiously asked as he gazed across the small table at Jack.

"Say nothing to no one about Warren and Pierce's little meeting," Jack instructed. "When you get to the bay, buddy up with my devious little brother. Wherever Warren goes, you try to go. Try to figure out everything he's got going on. Now you have to be careful," Jack warned. "Warren is pretty sly. You don't want him to find out what you're up to."

"What am I to do when I realize what's going on?" Thomas asked Jack sincerely. "I won't be seeing you for a while."

"You can write me," Jack suggested. "Just send the mail to yalls' address and I'll pick it up. While you're watching Warren, I'll be watching Pierce."

Thomas' smile had faded and his mind appeared to suddenly drift from the conversation.

"What's the matter?" Jack asked him.

"I don't know," replied the young man. "You know, it just don't feel right does it?"

"What doesn't feel right?" Jack then probed.

"Spying on your own flesh and blood," answered Thomas earnestly.

"Look, Thomas," Jack said, "family or not, if Warren is up to something wrong with Pierce, then something's got to be done. You do understand that don't you?"

"I understand," Thomas promised. "But it still don't make it seem right."

"No," Jack agreed, "it doesn't but you're going to find a lot of things in life just don't seem right."

The uncle-nephew team sipped their coffee for a few more moments in silence. They were each secretly brooding of Warren's activities with Pierce. Suddenly Thomas turned his train of thought from Warren to Jack. The young man was concerned about the loneliness Jack had obviously experienced over the years.

Jack had been raised in a close knit family and apparently enjoyed the busy life they had all once shared of raising crops and working cattle. Warren had lost that over one hand of cards though. It had been said that Jack so much wanted a son to carry on his name. That son was still born. Finally, it had also been said and was quite obvious Stella was the driving force behind a great man.

Thomas Wheeler had heard over his short years of how Stella had actually tamed the legendary Jack McKinley. It was she who had stopped the fighting and carousing Jack had once so actively participated in. Although for only a few years in Jack's life, it was Stella that had helped him see himself as someone capable of positive deeds. She had transformed Jack into a family man. Unfortunately she lost touch with the world and reality when the baby died, leaving Jack alone again.

"Jack," Thomas called.

Jack's sad blue eyes then focused upon the nephew he was slowly beginning to know. "Yea?" he replied in a crackling voice.

"Jack, do you ever see Stella?" The boy asked carefully.

"What brought that up?" Jack replied rhetorically.

"I don't know," Thomas admitted. "Well do you?"

For a lengthy while, Jack McKinley remained speechless. He didn't even appear to be in search for words to answer his inquisitive nephew. Instead, he slowly sipped the cup of black coffee he had just replenished.

Finally Thomas saw Jack's eyes water. Although the tear drops did not trickle, the lad knew they were there. He felt ashamed for having asked such a personal question. In fact, the young man felt so ashamed, he was too embarrassed to bring himself to apologize.

Neither of the two said anything for some time. Jack continued to sip his java as Thomas poured himself another cup.

"I saw her about six months ago," Jack finally said. "She is still as pretty as she was the first time I saw her, Thomas."

It was then Thomas saw his uncle smile as he had never seen before. It was not a big smile nor a happy smile, but a proud smile. The smile was also accented by the gentle dribble of a single tear down Jack McKinley's weather beaten cheek.

Thomas smiled at his uncle in attempt to offer support. He did not know what to say but a gentle smile was all Jack really needed.

"She's in Chatahoochee you know," Jack continued.

"Is she?" The young man replied.

"Yes," Jack said. "I see her a couple of times each year"

Again, silence prevailed as Jack McKinley and Thomas Wheeler sipped their coffee. Thomas was at a loss of words and Jack had much to say. There had been so many words he had kept within himself over the years but was unsure where to start.

Once more a sole teardrop trickled down Jack's cheek as he began to speak in a helpless voice. "You know, I never let her see me," he began. "Lord knows I want her to but I'm afraid it'll only bring back bad memories of losing the baby. Besides, the doctors say she's doing real good so I reckon she doesn't need me."

"I'll bet she thinks of you often, Jack," the boy replied. "Have you written to her?"

"No," Jack replied. "That'll probably set her off again, too."

Jack then began telling Thomas of the day he and Stella had met. The boy was amused by his uncle's stories for nearly one hour. Jack McKinley had softened in his nephew's company and the boy in his.

After much conversation that evening, Thomas excused himself to go home and finish preparing for his stay at Dead Man's Bay. As he walked out the door of his uncle's cabin, Jack called out to him.

"Yes sir?" Thomas replied.

"Be careful in Dead Man's Bay now," Jack instructed. "Watch out for your ma and little brother and sister. You'll have to look out after Old Amos too. You know how the folks are down at the bay."

"Yes sir," said Thomas with the return of his trademark smile.

"Oh, and one more thing," Jack added. "I don't want mama and papa involved in what ever it is that Warren is up to. They are good people and so is Warren's wife, Melanie. She does not need to be involved either."

"No problem," replied the young man as he began walking into the dark to board the old Chevrolet truck.

Chapter XI

There was a little bite of winter in the air the following morning. Thanksgiving was just around the corner so old man winter was right on schedule, Thomas thought. Thanksgiving in Dead Man's Bay, also known as Steinhatchee, was nothing unusual for Thomas' family. It had been a tradition through the years to spend the holiday there. Ever since James and Martha McKinley had married 1904, it was tradition to enjoy Florida's Gulf Coast on the particular holiday.

In the early years of the senior McKinley's marriage, Martha would enjoy a week of having returned to her roots. As for James, it was always special for him as well. He had never seen anything to match the beauty of the Steinhachee River dumping into those gulf stream waters he had often said.

Martha's father would often carry James out to fish when the couple visited her parents. As for Thomas, he too liked the gulf coast. He did not have an equal admiration though for it that his grandparents did however. It was just somewhere to go for the lad.

After Thomas finished milking the cow and feeding up, he stopped into Amos' quarters and made his counterpart a fresh pot of coffee. After a few minutes of casual conversation, the young man peered out of Amos' bedroom window. It was probably around seven in the morning. Much to his surprise and satisfaction, the Porters were boarding their car to leave.

In a rush, the young man slipped on his jacket and made it outside before Wilbur and Estelle Porter drove away.

"It was sure a pleasure to see ya'll again," Thomas called out with a cunning little smile.

Now go, he silently thought as Rose continued to give them peanut candy and cookies for their trip. After a few more minutes of farewells, the Porters were on their way home and the Wheelers could soon set off as well.

After going inside, Rose instructed Thomas to wake Allen and Nancy. After doing so, the four Wheelers set down to a delicious breakfast. Before the meal, Thomas returned thanks and asked God to be with his father and asked that he soon return him to them. Rose had prepared grits and eggs to go along with smoked sausages and biscuits. Cane syrup seemed to be the clincher for that particular meal though.

"Thomas," Rose said.

"Yes ma'am," her eldest replied.

"Where did you go last night?"

"I had to go see Jack," Thomas said.

"Whatever for?" Rose probed.

"Well you know Ma, I don't think Jack knows a whole lot about what to do around here and I had to remind him about keeping plenty of laying mash. You know, so the chickens will lay," explained the young man.

"Do you suppose Jack will figure out how to go about opening the feed sacks?" Rose replied with a sarcastic grin.

Naturally Thomas was not intending to mislead his mother. He did not feel it to be appropriate to share the information with her he had learned from Porter concerning Warren either. It did seem like he mentioned the laying mash to Jack anyway.

After excusing himself from the breakfast table, Thomas ventured outside to help Amos with his luggage. Thomas had already decided they would have everything packed and ready to go on the front porch so that when Jack arrived they could just put it all in his car.

"You have your stuff together?" The young man asked Amos.

"It's all together," Amos replied.

"Good," said Thomas. "I'll set it on the porch."

"I've got it," Amos insisted.

"No," Thomas demanded with a grin. "you know what Doc said. Looks like you'll be relying on me for a few days now don't it."

Amos only shook his head and looked at Thomas. It was as if the poor old fellow was awaiting pure mischief to exhume from the lad. Of course Amos knew if he stuck around Thomas long enough, witnessing mischief in progress was inevitable.

It wasn't long before Rose and the children had all their luggage outside as well. The four Wheelers and Amos enjoyed a peaceful rock in the chairs along the front porch as they awaited Jack's arrival. Rocking was meant to be among the pleasantries in rural North Florida life but too much crowded each of their minds. First and foremost was the fate of Charles Wheeler. Of course there was the Pierce situation as well. As for Thomas, he would secretly brood over the idea of his own flesh and blood being seen with the likes of Scott Pierce.

There was still no sign of Pierce returning to his place. He was evidently still at the mouth of the Suwannee, Thomas thought. The lad then couldn't help but wonder what business would carry such a man there.

Journey of Truth

"I see Jack a comin'," Amos muttered out.

"O.K. children," Rose instructed, "get ready to get into the car.

In compliance, Allen and Nancy did as their mother had asked. It was all either of them could do to lug the heavy bags their mother had instructed them to carry. They did manage however. They were rather adorable in the nautical style clothing Rose had dressed them in.

Nancy wore a navy blue dress with a white collar. There were also huge white buttons along the front with a white belt at the waist. She was a rather elegant looking young lady.

Allen on the other hand looked like a little boy waiting to get dirty. He was however quite handsome in his little sailor suit. The straw hat upon his head was a touch of Florida Cracker class.

As Jack rolled to a stop, the five soon to be travelers began loading the car. As they loaded their belongings, Rose reiterated Jack's instructions to be carried out during her absence.

"Oh and one more thing," Rose said in a monotone voice. "Thomas is awful concerned about the chickens having plenty laying of mash."

"Oh," Jack replied.

"Why sure," Rose continued. "Didn't he go to specifically tell you that last night?"

As Thomas smiled Jack stuttered. "Yes I, I bel-believe he did," Jack finally said.

Rose then looked at Thomas and smiled. It was not a happy smile. It was instead a "you can't fool me" smile.

As they drove off, Thomas looked across the land his family had once owned. For the first time since Pierce had returned, Thomas felt he and Jack were on the right track in getting rid of their foe. Thomas knew he was up to something. He also felt sure with him and Amos in Steinhachee and Jack in Suwannee County, together they would determine Pierce's activities and let the authorities take him down. There was a complication though. If Warren was involved it was sure to take him down as well. Thomas didn't mind and Jack didn't mind taking Warren down. The one thing that complicated the whole matter so was they wanted to protect Warren's wife and parents.

The trip was to take approximately two hours. Thomas promised his siblings if they would be good, he would stop the car in Mayo and buy them a soda water each. They had done just as he asked so when they reached the small town of Mayo, Florida he stopped and lived up to his end of the bargain.

While inside Harrell's General Merchantile, Thomas had the opportunity to see his old buddy Mut Jacobson. To most folks, Mut was no more than a no count river rat. He had never held steady employment in his life. It was no secret though that Mut would paddle moonshine up and down river. He was not a known maker of the stuff but had no reservations in distributing it for the makers. Old Mut was even known to drink it as well.

He was a dirty man and usually presented himself unshaven. His dark oily hair was curly and never seemed in any sort of order. Mut wore one set of clothes. They served as his summer and winter outfit. It was doubtful he washed them even for the seasons' change.

"Hey there, Mut," Thomas called out.

"Well, Thomas Wheeler," Mut replied, "been doin' any fishin'?"

"Yes I have," the lad boasted. "But all the big ones are getting away Mut."

"Well now," Mut said in his deep voice. "You just come along with Old Mut one day and I'll show you how to keep the big ones."

"Now Mut," Thomas began with a smile. "Surely you don't think my ma's going to trust me off fishing with you do you?"

"Hey," Mut hastily replied, "I ain't all that bad now. At least I ain't as bad as those fellows I saw a couple of days ago. You know 'em Thomas. It's that Pierce boy that just got out of prison. Thomas they was dynamitin' fish and I tell you that just boiled my blood."

"You don't say," Thomas said.

"That's a fact," confirmed Mut. "That ain't no way to fish."

Interesting, the young man thought as he bid Mut farewell and paid for his siblings drinks. Thomas couldn't help but wonder if dynamite was the connection with his uncle, Warren. Nonetheless dynamite wasn't healthy, especially in the hands of a crazed lunatic.

Finally, they were out of Mayo and on their way to Steinhachee. In effort to keep the children from getting restless, Rose would warn them of a deer around every corner they approached. Much to her surprise, they did see two large bucks.

Finally the salty air prevailed. It was not an unfamiliar scent to no one of the five aboard Jack's thirty-four model Ford coupe. Attention was then turned from deer to the unique boats they were about to see.

At last, Thomas wheeled the car into the drive of the home occupied by his grandparents, aunt, and uncle.

Chapter XII

Bay Fish Camp was the name of the McKinley business in Steinhachee. Martha McKinley's parents, Ruben and Isabelle Williams had built the small camp. Through the years the business grew slowly and maintained itself.

Recently the business had grown quite well. Due to vehicles being able to transport seafood at greater distances, the Bay Fish Camp's clientele had certainly enlarged. James, Martha, and Melanie McKinley all possessed sound business minds. Warren at least had the personality.

The camp was almost like a compound. It consisted of approximately five acres. Behind it was the tranquil Steinhachee River. The home and the camp were side by side. Between them stood cabbage palms. Between the compound and river was a dike consisting of rock. The dike was approximately four feet in height. It was perfect for little Wheeler children to play pirates. Indeed the game was quite fitting for the locality.

The house was a bungalow style home. It was a great deal larger than the Wheeler home in Suwannee County. Fresh white paint was always apparent throughout the camp. The house as well as the other buildings steadily remained clean and in good repair. Thomas especially liked the four piece setting of wicker furniture near the dam behind the house.

Between the house and the river just offset from the wicker furniture setting was the small cottage Warren and Melanie occupied. It looked like a tiny version of the large bungalow. The cottage contained only a kitchenette, bedroom, and a bathroom.

On the front porch of the Steinhachee McKinley home were six white rocking chairs. Screen enclosed the porch as well. As the four Wheelers and Amos drove into the drive, they found James and Martha McKinley setting in the rocking chairs sipping lemonade. Melanie McKinley accompanied them.

Melanie quickly exited the porch and hugged Rose as she emerged from Jack's coupe.

"Oh, Rose," Melanie began, "it is good to see you. I am so proud you all have come down to the bay."

Melanie was a slender lady who consistently wore cheerful cotton dresses. The dresses perhaps complimented her simple beauty. Even during the winter months she would wear colors that might be more appropriate for summer. When the cold air was a bit too much, she would put on one of her many sweaters. Melanie's complexion was usually very tanned due to the constant exposure of Florida's Gulf Coast sun. During the work day, she would place her long brown hair up into a bun on the back of her head. After the day's work was complete, she would allow it to fall to it's natural state.

James and Martha perhaps looked a little more typical Suwannee County, Florida. He had never given up his solid khaki outfits nor had she given up her solid colored dresses. The Senior McKinley's had been a reputable couple in James' native Suwannee County. Although they had never really entertained the thought moving to Dead Man's Bay, they had began spending much of their time there prior to Warren's ill-famed poker game.

Perhaps James and Martha McKinley had been lucky for they actually had two places they thought of as home. Warren had always seen Steinhachee as his eventual home even as a child. Rose on the other hand had always seemed to think of the McKinley land in Suwannee County as home. As for Jack, he never totally felt at home anywhere. Although his love for Steinhachee and Suwannee County was obvious, Jack had also seemed unsettled much of his life.

As Melanie walked Rose to the porch, James and Martha McKinley also made their way outside to welcome the Wheeler clan. Martha hugged the children and Rose as James picked at them. He was just being a typical grandpa.

Sir Thomas did not accompany his family inside. He on the other hand assisted Amos to his quarters. The older black gentleman had visited those same quarters many times over the years. He, too, referred to the Bay as his second home.

As Thomas accompanied his counterpart to the little room attached to the fish camp, he heard his grandpa call out.

"Thomas Wheeler," James called.

"Hey, Grandpa," Thomas shouted as he waved and grinned largely.

"Mr. McKinley," acknowledged Amos as he also smiled.

"Hello, Amos," said James McKinley. "It's so good to see you again. Rose tells me you have a full time job keeping Thomas here straight."

"Well Mr. McKinley," Amos replied modestly. "I think Thomas makes it his business to keep Old Amos here straight."

The three gentlemen smiled in accordance. James thanked Amos for going to the Bay with Rose and the children and then asked Thomas to accompany him out on the flats the following morning.

Needless to say, Thomas readily agreed. Catching red fish and speckled trout rated right at the top of the young man's priorities.

After insuring Amos was settled into his room, the lad started the short walk back over to the house. He then saw his uncle, Warren sitting out at the wicker furniture. Warren was indeed a dandy looking character. He always was. Warren McKinley was in his mid-thirties with a distinctive hint of gray in his dark hair. The suit he wore was almost impossible to distinguish from his others. They were all dark in color with faint pin striping. The material was of a tropical lightweight and the small lapels were always immaculate.

Thomas had to stand there for a moment and appreciate the man. Although he never cared an awful lot for Warren, he did admire the way he presented himself. Even Warren's shoes were untainted at any given time. That was a lot said for a man that supposedly made his living in a fish camp in Dead Man's Bay, also know as Steinhachee, Florida.

Not only did Warren always look impressive, he also knew how to handle himself delicately around business associates. The young man noted the way his uncle sat poised. Although he offered the appearance of comfort, he appeared to be totally focused on what the other gentleman had to offer in their conversation as well.

Warren McKinley was a much smaller man than his brother Jack, in stature. The younger Warren weighed no more than one hundred seventy pounds and was five foot ten inches in height.

Thomas observed Warren closely. He sat with his right leg casually crossed over his left. While he rested his left arm on the wicker arm chair he occupied, Warren gently held a cigarette with his right hand. Resting on his left knee was the small brimmed Stetson straw hat. It was a stylish hat. The back of the brim was turned up while the sides extended nearly straight out and the front was turned down just a tad.

More than one hundred feet separated Thomas from Warren. Therefore the lad did not find it necessary to interfere with his uncle's business. His intentions were to slip away unnoticed, but he did not.

A small single engine plane flew directly over the fish camp at less than three hundred feet in altitude. Warren McKinley held a fascination beyond words for airplanes and simply could not resist observing that particular plane as the pilot continued his northern course along the beautiful coast line.

As Warren watched the small aircraft meet the horizon, he focused on Thomas Wheeler.

"Thomas," Warren called out, "I didn't know you all were here yet. Please come down here."

Slowly the young man meandered toward the river's bank where Warren sat leisurely.

"Hello Uncle Warren," the boy said in a docile manner while sporting his trademark smile.

Warren McKinley stood and extended his hand addressing Thomas Wheeler not as a child but as a man.

"We're glad you all came, Thomas," Warren said. "I would like for you to meet Mr. Willis."

The gentleman whom Warren had been engaged with in conversation then rose to his feet and shook the young man's hand. He was cordial enough although Thomas did notice he appeared slightly provoked at having been disturbed by a lad while discussing business.

"This is my nephew, Thomas Wheeler," Warren explained to Willis. "And this is Mr. Willis," he told Thomas.

Although neither Thomas nor Mr. Willis were interested, they acted so just the same. Warren informed his nephew that Mr. Willis had recently moved into Florida from New York. They were currently discussing the possibility of Willis contracting a fish route for the Bay Fish Camp.

After the brief greetings and conversation, Thomas made his way up the small hill to the bungalow in which his family was to stay for a while. The large rooms had always been impressive to him. Perhaps the thing that impressed him even more was the coastal appeal the home possessed.

To begin with, it was lighted extremely well. There was plenty of windows in the bungalow and they were often kept open. Thomas was especially dazzled by the window screens over the outside of the windows. He found it truly relaxing to set with the windows open and allow the coastal breeze to engulf him into it's web of contentment.

Martha McKinley had offered her own refined tastes to incorporate their home furnishings with the natural beauty of the gulf to offer a decor of elegance and comfort. Much of the pictures in the McKinley's Steinhachee home were those of the gulf's natural habitat. A few decorative models of ships were also on display about the house.

Thomas stood in the living room marveling the latest boat his grandparents had added to their collection. He could hear everyone else back in the detached kitchen and along the breezeway that extended along the kitchen.

"Where is Thomas?" The young man heard his grandmother ask.

"Knowing Thomas Wheeler," his mother began, "he's liable to be out at sea aggravating the sharks."

The young man smiled with dignity. He was happy to know his mother found him capable of making even the sharks miserable.

"Thomas Wheeler's in the living room, Grandma," he politely shouted.

Immediately, Martha McKinley journeyed into the living room and joined her oldest grandson.

"Thomas," she began, "I sure am glad you are here. I think Uncle Warren needs a good strong fellow like yourself in the fish camp. And of course Amos is going to be a big help as well."

"Old Amos isn't going to be much help for a while," Thomas quickly informed his grandmother. "You know he got his ribs busted. Any heavy lifting anybody around here was plannin' for him to do, let me know. I'll do it my own self."

Such reaction from anyone else at Thomas' tender age might have shocked an adult. Nobody was shocked at such a response from Thomas however. That was just his character. He held much admiration and love for Amos and although he might not be willing to tell the old fellow, his actions spoke much louder than words.

"I'm frying up some chicken and cooking grits and biscuits," Martha then told the unique young man with a loving smile. "I think we need to get Amos some just as soon as it gets ready."

Thomas' big grin was worth more to her than all the money in the world. It made her happy to see the young man care so much for others.

"Thank you," Thomas replied modestly, "we sure do appreciate it, Grandma."

Chapter XIII

The next morning, Jack McKinley awoke just a little bit disoriented. It was the first night he had not slept in his cabin in over ten years. Although raised in the very house he had just awaken, he was simply not at home. Even in an incoherent state of mind, he maintained the realization that the old house still served as a happy home to his sister's family.

After getting a pot of coffee started, Jack got dressed and prepared himself for the day. Finally, he walked out to the kitchen and poured himself a cup of strong black coffee from the pot. Jack McKinley slowly sipped the piping coffee as he walked out to greet the crisp, cool morning.

He then sat down on the porch and observed the busy squirrels gathering the pecans. Thomas' old hound dog sauntered up to Jack and attempted to cold nose him as the few cattle began to bellow in hopes of being fed.

"Get dog," scorned Jack. "I'll feed you later but I'm going to nurse a touch of hang over now."

As Jack McKinley set on the front porch and sipped his coffee, he became a little angry. As he continued to think about the whole Pierce situation, he became madder and madder. Perhaps he was most angry with himself because he knew ten years prior no man alive would have gone into Suwannee County and pulled such a stunt with any family of Jack McKinley.

"Come on dog and I'll feed you," he said in a much kinder voice. "You need to eat good 'cause it's looking like me and you've got our work cut out for us."

Jack then fed the livestock and rode about the remaining forty acres of his families land in the old Chevrolet truck. As he drove the perimeter of the fence, he could tell Pierce and company were back from their river excursion. Initially, Jack wanted to drive straight across the field and set things straight. He did not do that because he had not made it thus far in life being totally ignorant.

Instead of going on the rampage he really preferred, Jack rode into town so that he could buy the laying mash Thomas was evidently so concerned about. Before doing so, Jack stopped in at the Suwannee Cafe where he thoroughly enjoyed pancakes, sausage, eggs, and grits.

Many of the patrons whispered among themselves, "Is that Jack McKinley?"

"Yes," others would reply. "I didn't think he sobered up long enough to eat."

Although Jack overheard some of the old timers, he made no comment. The way he figured, he deserved it. That still didn't take any of the hurt away. Quietly, he completed his meal, paid the cashier and walked toward the door.

"Jack McKinley," he heard a man say, "I hear you just a no good drunk now."

"I reckon so," Jack replied softly as he turned and saw Horace Brooker standing in his overalls.

"That nephew of yours and his colored man are a couple of fools," Horace then said sarcastically.

Silence prevailed for a moment among the onlookers. Horace Brooker had just said something that no man should ever say to another. Furthermore, he had said it to Jack McKinley.

Jack stood straight and looked hard into Brooker's eyes. He would occasionally take a split second to break eye contact with him only to see what Brooker's hands were doing. Finally a faint smile of pride overcame Jack.

"That is some boy," Jack said. "A fine boy. And I'll tell you right now Brooker if I ever hear you belittle him again I will beat you half to death. As for me, I'm whatever people say. I've ruined my own self, but I'll be blessed if I'll let anybody ruin that boy, especially you."

"Now wait a minute, Jack," Brooker muttered.

"And the same goes for Amos too." Jack retorted. "You will not belittle him either. Do I make myself clear?"

With a look of defeat, Brooker replied, "I didn't mean no......."

"And I won't mean any harm when I beat you to a pulp," Jack interrupted and then exited the restaurant.

"Looks like Jack McKinley still ain't nobody to be messed up with," commented one of the old timers.

Jack was fully awoke by the time he walked out of the Suwannee Cafe. He then fired up the Chevrolet truck and rode across to Guthrie's Farm Supply where he purchased laying mash and a few fence posts. Although the fence posts had not been left on his list of instructions, Jack deemed it necessary to replace a few old ones.

While at Guthries, Jack became amazed at how long it had been since he had seen so many people. It was almost as if Jack was becoming saddened as he thought of the many years he had wasted. He was however delighted that most everyone appeared to be pleased to see him.

As Jack was beginning his drive out of town, he decided to drop by Mason's and buy himself an R.C. Cola and a Moon Pie. Gently, he rolled the truck into what he considered a parking place just across the street from Mason's and began walking over to the store.

"Hey, you can't park there," a stranger yelled to him from across the street.

"I'm sorry," Jack replied. "I'll move it," he continued with a smile.

"That is not good enough," the stranger insisted. He then asked in a very sarcastic manner, "Is your name Wheeler?"

"McKinley's my name, Jack McKinley. Who wants to know?" Jack then replied just as cynical.

"Pierce," the stranger said confidently. "Scott Pierce."

"Are you Pierce?" Jack asked as he walked steadily toward the stranger.

"No, I work for him," the stranger admitted.

By then, Jack McKinley was within two feet of the man. He was indeed a large man. Although he was not very tall, the stranger was extremely muscular. Jack could tell by his accent the stranger was not local. More than likely he was out of the Chicago area, Jack thought. That within itself further angered Jack McKinley. Horace Brooker was a pain in the neck but at least he was a local pain. The last thing Jack needed was an outsider coming in and starting trouble.

The punch was sudden and it was extremely hard. Jack's right fist found the forehead of Pierce's goon. Immediately, the goon fell to the ground in an incoherent state. Jack then walked over into the small alley next to Mason's where a pail of rain water sat. As Jack walked toward the pail he rubbed his right fist with his left hand. He then picked up the water, walked over to the goon and poured the water in his face. The stranger on the ground then began coughing uncontrollably.

"You can tell Pierce that Jack McKinley wants to see him," Jack said abruptly as he threw the pail on the goon's chest. "Put the bucket back in the alley when you get up."

Jack then calmly walked into Mason's and bought his R.C. Cola and Moon Pie. As he exited Mason's the beaten man was sitting in an upright position on the ground with a confused look about his face. Jack simply tipped his hat as he walked by.

On his way back to the Wheeler Place, Jack dropped by his cabin just to check things out there. While at the cabin, he decided to walk on down to The Club Palmetto where Zeb was cleaning up from the previous night.

"Good night last night?" Jack asked as he walked in to the juke.

"How do you do, Jack?" Zeb said. "We did O.K.. Is everything worked out with Miss Rose?"

Jack poured himself a cup of coffee and took a sip before answering.

"Not yet Zeb," he said. "And I don't know how long before it's going to work out either."

"Sorry to hear that," Zeb commented. "Anything I can do?"

"Just keep an eye on the cabin and see after my part in this place if you don't mind," Jack replied.

"Well, I don't know," Zeb began slowly. "You know I have all I can do as it is."

Jack quickly looked at Zeb with a strong display of disappointment and Zeb began to laugh.

"Jack McKinley," Zeb said, "you know I don't mind doing anything you ask me to do. If anything else comes along you need done, just you tell me and I'll do it."

"I appreciate it," Jack replied. "I also want to tell you what is going on in case something was to happen to me, Zeb."

"Oh they ain't nothin' gonna happen to you, Jack," Zeb snapped.

"I know," Jack said with a subtle smile, "but I would still like to tell you just the same."

Jack then spent the next hour sharing the pot of coffee with Zeb and filling him in on the whole Pierce ordeal. He told Zeb everything from Warren's infamous poker game to Rose and her children going to the bay. He failed to report to Zeb on his encounter with Pierce's goon in town. Finally, Jack told Zeb about how he was disappointed in his own self for allowing such a thing happen.

"You know, Zeb," Jack commented, "Pierce wouldn't have pulled this stunt ten years ago."

Zeb just smiled and assured Jack he would assist him any way he possibly could.

As Jack walked out of The Club Palmetto, Zeb called out, "Hey, Jack."

"Yea?" Jack replied.

"You had better put some ice on that hand," Zeb stated earnestly.

After conversing with Zeb, Jack cranked up the Chevrolet truck and headed for the Wheeler place. He drove at a leisurely pace and reflected on the past. Mostly thinking of his parents and Stella, Jack made a secret vow to spend time with them all should he successfully bring the Pierce problem to an end.

Upon returning to his sister's farm, Jack began assessing the grounds from all angles as he anticipated a showdown with Pierce and his whole gang.

Chapter XIV

While Jack had already spent a couple of days anxiously awaiting Scott Pierce to fulfill his invitation to personally meet him, Thomas was becoming increasingly busy at Bay Fish Camp. He had not forgotten his mission of spying on his uncle, Warren McKinley in the least. By being at the camp as much as possible, he would understand it's operations better and could more easily identify Warren's legitimate business acquaintances. Furthermore, he could look after Amos better.

As for the duties bestowed upon Amos and Thomas, they were really very limited. They assisted in unloading boats and loading trucks. At the end of each day, they would wash out the floors and dispose of the fish scraps.

That particular evening, Warren and Melanie were also in the scaling house. It had been an unusually busy day and they were working late assisting the less experienced Amos and Thomas.

"Thomas," Warren called out happily.

"Yes sir?" replied Thomas.

"I have to go up to Jug Island tomorrow afternoon to look at some nets and thought maybe you would like to go," suggested Warren.

"No, thank you," answered Thomas.

"Why not?" Warren asked with a tone of genuine disappointment.

"No particular reason," replied the young man. "I'm just not much on going places for little reason."

Warren truly looked sad and rejected by the nephew he was attempting to know better.

"Maybe some other time," Warren said with a forced smile.

No comment was made by Amos or Melanie during the verbal exchange of Warren and Thomas. Shortly there after, Warren drove down to a local marina where he would buy himself and Melanie coffee to have in their cottage. Melanie went out for her afternoon walk along the bank of the Steinhachee River.

"You know, Amos," Thomas said, "I think you and me need to go up river a ways and catch us a mess of bream. You and me can have our own little fish fry then."

Amos just smiled easily as he and Thomas cleaned the wooden floors inside the fish camp. Amos hosed the floor and Thomas scrubbed it with a broom. All the while, Thomas was thinking of his father.

"We ought to be able to go up there in the mornin'," Amos said. "Reckon Mr. McKinley will let us take that little boat and kicker of his'n."

"Why sure," the lad replied. "You know, Amos, Grandpa's a pretty good sort of a fellow."

Again, Amos just smiled as his young counterpart continued to scrub the floors. The sounds of boats about the water gave them each hope. At least they did not feel as alone at the bay as they had as of late in their native Suwannee County.

"Amos," Thomas called out.

"Yes, Thomas," Amos patiently replied.

"Do you ever think about Pa much?" The lad outright asked his best friend and mentor.

"I sho 'nuff do," Amos replied with a pleasant smile.

"Do you pray for him, Amos?" The lad continued to probe.

"Every day," Amos assured his sidekick and protege. "I know it ain't easy for you and your ma to talk about so I don't bring it up too much. Oh but I'm always thinkin' 'bout Mr. Charles. Dat's a good man, Thomas Wheeler. You just aim to be like him and you'll do just fine. Yes sir."

The young man continued to work as he held a serious look on his face. Amos knew he was in deep concentration but had no idea Thomas' thoughts had turned to spying on his uncle.

After the two men completed their work, Amos journeyed into his small quarters for a sip of whisky he had slipped down from Suwannee County. Thomas made his way to the river bank and sat upon his favorite rock. There he would watch the boats, large and small come in from the salty gulf. Others, the lad would peacefully observe return to the sometimes relentless waters of the gulf. He too yearned to some-day travel out to sea.

Thomas observed a very small vessel making it's way up river for a while. Soon after, he turned his attention to the larger boats. He did however allow his attention to return to the small skiff. By then the skiff was docked along some rocks on the opposite side of the river.

A man got out of the boat and walked up onto the bank with a bad limp. Since the river is not a very wide river, the young man could distinguish much of the stranger's details. He possessed the looks of a true pirate. The typical flat topped black sailor's hat he wore appeared authentic enough from the distance the lad had to look. His left arm was gone. Instead of a hand extending beyond his shirt sleeve, a hook was there. The distance was just too great for Thomas to make out any detailed facial features.

Thomas attempted not to stare for he had been taught it was rude to do so. He was however unable to refrain from doing so. Once the stranger realized the young man was staring at him, he quickly returned to his skiff and headed back down river full speed. As he turned his skiff in the river, to return downstream, Thomas was able to tell a little more about him. His face was bearded. The young man also realized the stranger wore a patch over his left eye as well.

"Well hello Thomas," Melanie said.

"Good afternoon," the lad replied with a smile.

"Do you like the boats?" Melanie then asked.

"Yes ma'am," Thomas said. "I reckon a boat to folks down here is what a mule or a tractor is to folks back home."

"I suppose so," Melanie replied in laughter. "Thomas, I want you to feel like this is your home too. I know it isn't Suwannee County but you belong here just as much as Warren and I or anyone else for that matter."

"Yes ma'am," Thomas replied quietly and without expression as he held a small flat rock in his hand. "I guess I'm just more used to the Suwannee River and farmland."

The young man then stood and skipped the rock into the Steinhachee River. It bounced off the water four times before plummeting to the river's bed.

"Hey!" Melanie shouted. "You're pretty good but I'll bet I can skip this one five times."

She then bent over and picked up a rock without much shape. After looking it over, she showed it to Thomas.

"How much?" Thomas asked with a returning grin.

"Two bits," she replied.

"You're on," agreed the young man as Melanie spun around and released the rock to skip about the top of the river.

The shapeless rock did not stop at five bounces. Melanie had skipped it six times across the top of the water.

"Where did a woman learn to skip rock like that?" Thomas asked candidly.

"What do you mean?" Melanie replied in laughter with a failed attempt to sound sarcastic.

"You are good at skipping rock," Thomas outright admitted.

"When you live with Warren McKinley, you learn to do things like skipping rock," Melanie explained.

The young man appeared puzzled. He was unsure what his aunt meant by such a statement. In all honesty the lad actually thought she meant Warren was an enthusiast of skipping rock. As he closely studied the river, silence overtook their conversation and Melanie also began studying the flowing water.

"I have always loved this place," Melanie finally said.

Thomas acted as if he did not hear what she said as he immediately asked what she meant by the comment of Warren and skipping rock.

Melanie smiled softly. She then found a spot of her own to set down next to Thomas on the river's bank.

"Warren McKinley is a good man Thomas," she began. "Sometimes I think maybe he is just too good. Warren has ideas about business that are sometimes too incredible. He wants to make lots of money just so his whole family can have plenty. I know a lot of folks don't believe in Warren but I do. I know one day his ship's going to come in Thomas. I know a lot of people don't care a lot for him and I have a feeling you don't but I wish you would just give him a chance. Will you Thomas? He loves you so much."

The young man couldn't say much. She was right. He didn't care all that much for Warren McKinley but how could he tell his pleading aunt that.

"I'll try," the young man replied as he walked away searching for the company of Amos.

"Thomas," Melanie called out.

"Yes ma'am?" the lad replied.

With a tear trickling down her tanned cheek she said, "Warren loves Jack very much too."

Thomas then looked up in the yard and watched his own brother at play with their sister, Nancy. It was then that the words of Melanie began to hit closer to home for the young man. He made no reply. Instead, he simply addressed Warren's wife with a comforting smile of hope.

After retreating to the quarters of one Amos Washington, Thomas began weighing his conversation with Melanie. Perhaps she was right. Maybe he should give Warren a chance but the lad could not forget what Mr. Porter had told him about Warren's rendezvous with Pierce.

"What is on your mind now?" Amos candidly asked his young protege.

"I don't know Amos," the boy began. "I just wish we were back at the place where we ought to be."

"Well," Amos began with an understanding smile, "it just ain't that easy boy. Your Uncle Jack's got all that under control. I don't think me and you needs to be a gettin' tangled up with this Pierce fellow so why don't we just wait it out a few more days."

"I wish Pa was here," Thomas said with much confidence. "If he was home he would go ahead and put an end to all this Pierce trouble. I don't see why me and you and Jack can't."

"You sort of like your Uncle Jack, don't you?" Amos asked Thomas.

"What brought on that question?" Thomas replied.

"Oh I don't know," Amos said, "but you do, don't you?"

"Jack's alright," Thomas admitted. "He's just a little head strong you know."

As Amos walked over to the small cabinet in the tiny kitchen area of his quarters to replace his bottle, he turned and looked at Thomas through the corner of his eyes.

"A little headstrong, huh? Where on Earth you reckon he gets that from? You know, Thomas Wheeler, you is a little headstrong your own self. I never could understand where you and your ma and Jack got that from. Mr. and Mrs. McKinley ain't never been that way and you didn't get it from your pa."

Thomas just smiled as he observed his mentor at work. Periodically Amos would have to so call straighten Thomas out. Sometimes Thomas would intentionally get Amos started. The young man believed Amos needed to feel useful in such an area.

"You are right," Thomas said. "I'm a little headstrong my own self."

"You don't seem to like Warren all that well. Now why is that?" Amos continued to probe his protege as he began packing his pipe with the fragrant tobacco Rose especially enjoyed smelling.

"Warren?" Thomas answered in an evasive manner.

"Yea," Amos continued, "don't you like Warren?"

"I don't know," Thomas said shrugging his shoulders. "He just seems a little different."

Amos then lit his pipe and after a few initial draws, he inhaled deep. He then looked at Thomas quite seriously. After a moment, he sat down in front of the young man and leaned forward.

"Thomas," Amos began, "your Uncle Warren might seem hard to understand. He always did. I'm a gonna tell you somethin' 'bout dat man though. He's hurt more than anybody can imagine over the years. He wishes more than anything that him and your uncle, his brother Jack McKinley, could act like brothers ought to act. He don't have a brother so please, boy, let him have a nephew."

Thomas knew Amos was right and he knew Melanie had been right also. That didn't change the fact of what he had heard from Porter concerning his caring Uncle Warren though.

Shortly thereafter, supper was served in the bungalow. Seated at the head of the table was James McKinley. To his left was Martha and then Nancy. Next to Nancy was Rose. At the other end of the table was Warren. To his immediate left was Melanie. Seated between Melanie and Thomas was the youngest Mr. Wheeler, Allen. Needless to say, the dining room was rather roomy to accommodate such a sizable dinner table.

As the family all got situated around the table, James McKinley looked at his youngest grandson and smiled.

"Allen," he began. "I wonder if you would be so kind to ask the Lord to bless this food?"

Allen began to pray. In fact it started to look like the little fellow was going to preach. Finally the famished Thomas interrupted.

"Amen," Thomas said softly to no avail.

Allen continued to pray.

"Amen," Thomas again said.

"I'll do my own prayin'," scolded Allen.

To say the least, it was difficult for the adults to keep their composure. A touch of adolescent humor had once again blessed the McKinley household.

After Allen's lengthy blessing the family began devouring swamp cabbage, hushpuppies, baked sweet potatoes, and mullet. Needless to say, a jar of guava jelly was on the table to enrich the flavor of the hushpuppies. That savory combination would readily suffice as a dessert.

"Allen," Warren said, "I thought maybe you would like to go to Jug Island with me tomorrow after lunch."

"He can't," Thomas answered hastily. "Today I bought him a new little boat he needs to play with. Besides, I thought maybe your offer still stood for me to go."

Warren smiled in acceptance. "Thomas, nothing would make me happier," he said.

Warren knew nothing of Melanie's conversation with Thomas nor would he ever know. He knew nothing of Amos' conversation with the lad either. It was not necessary for Warren to know.

After everyone was well into their meals, Thomas took a break from his eating.

"Grandpa," said Thomas in a very gentle manner.

"Yes, Thomas?" replied James McKinley.

"Have you ever seen a strange lookin' sort of a fellow out in the river?" Thomas asked. "I saw him in a small green skiff."

"Did he say something to you?" Rose immediately asked.

"Oh no, Ma," Thomas quickly replied. "I have just never seen anyone quite like that fellow before. Kind of scary in a way."

"Scary?" Martha asked out of pure curiosity.

"Yes, ma'am, Thomas continued. "He had a hook for a hand and a bad limp. He looked like a real pirate to me."

"Mama?" Nancy asked. "Did Thomas really see that?"

Rose Wheeler gave her eldest child an unpleasant look. She then looked around the table for a moment and said, "There is no telling what Thomas Wheeler will see."

"Especially down here," James said. "We do get some strange characters through time and again."

Conversation soon turned to an old family friend. Thomas however remained quiet as he ate and continued to contemplate the peculiar character he had seen in a green skiff earlier that day. There was just something about the man that captivated Thomas Wheeler.

Chapter XV

As Warren drove the panel truck owned by The Bay Fish Camp toward Jug Island, Thomas quietly rode shotgun. The virgin timber stood very noble about the forest bordering the Gulf of Mexico. The young man observed the trees' gentle sways as the coastal breeze forced them to wave in the various fowls of the seas.

"What do you think of this part of the world, Thomas?" Warren asked.

"Fine I guess," Thomas replied. "It sure ain't Suwannee County but I reckon it'll do."

Warren smiled patiently. He understood his nephew's love for Suwannee County for, he, too had the same love for their native county.

"I am glad you could come with me today," Warren commented over the hum of the old six cylinder engine.

"You aiming to buy some fishing nets?" Thomas asked.

"I'm going to look at them," Warren answered. "One of the fellows that brings us fish needs some new nets for his boat." Warren then smiled and said, "I thought we would buy them for him."

"Why don't he buy his own?" The young man rightfully asked.

"Well," Warren began, "he's a little down on his luck right now and I figured it to be the right thing to do."

That statement was unsettling to Thomas Wheeler. He thought of how hard his mother and Amos had worked on their farm and to his knowledge Warren McKinley had offered no support whatsoever. To think they were his own blood kin and here he was helping a mere business acquaintance.

Warren continued to drive and Thomas continued to be quiet. They were only a couple of miles from Jug Island when Warren stopped the truck and pointed out into the palmetto bushes.

"Hey look," he said, "it's deer. He looks hurt."

Thomas suddenly perked up as he too saw the deer hobble about one hundred fifty feet into the woods and fall down. Thomas looked at the mangled creature and then looked helplessly at his uncle.

"We gotta help it, Warren," the lad pleaded.

With a grim look of sincerity, Warren rubbed his lower left cheek with his right hand and squinted his eyes.

"We'll see," Warren said as he reached for the shotgun.

"No!" Thomas yelled. "You ain't a gonna shoot 'em, Warren. That just wouldn't be right."

Warren McKinley knew if the deer had been badly hurt, a lethal gunshot would be the only humane treatment for it. Thomas also knew that. Warren however chose to leave the gun in the truck as Thomas had wished.

Although autumn was upon them and Thanksgiving was rapidly approaching, the Florida heat was ever so present that very day. Warren removed his hat and wiped the sweat from his eyes and forehead with an ironed white handkerchief from his pocket.

"Come along," Warren said to Thomas as he meandered toward the injured deer.

"No," the young man replied. "I think I will wait here."

"Very well," Warren replied as he continued his steady pace into the pine trees, cabbage palms, and palmetto.

From the truck, Thomas watched him. At last he saw Warren get within ten feet of the deer and stop. He then saw Warren slowly look behind him and cease all movement.

"Thomas," Warren softly called out, "bring the gun."

"No, Warren," Thomas pleaded as his little heart pounded rapidly, "don't make me do it."

"Thomas, I said bring the gun!" Warren repeated in a more demanding tone.

Thomas then removed the gun from the truck and mumbled to himself as he began to walk out into the North Florida forest. When Thomas got within sixty feet of his uncle, Warren gently called his name.

"Yes sir?" the unhappy Thomas answered.

"Walk very slowly and do not rattle the palmetto," Warren warned.

After a few more steps, Thomas understood Warren's behavior. The young man began to hear the snake's rattlers steady rattle. The diamond back was only two feet from Warren's feet. The venomous serpent lay coiled and continued to sing it's rattlers. Thomas knew the snake was positioned and ready to strike. The young man also knew if Warren moved the snake would strike. The only feasible solution was shoot the rattlesnake. To further complicate matters, Thomas stood in an extremely poor place to make the shot. A palmetto bush was between Thomas and the snake. Unfortunately, the young man could not risk moving any closer out of fear of the snake striking.

Warren's position wasn't exactly comfortable either. He was sweating heavily and could not even wipe the sweat from his face. His own heart rate had became extremely accelerated.

"O.K., Thomas," Warren said in a trembling voice. "Shoot the snake."

"What if I hit you?" Thomas asked earnestly.

"You probably will," Warren replied. "The buckshot is going to scatter but I had rather get hit by a stray bead than his fangs."

No more was said. The shot was fired and the rattling stopped as the dead snake began a sadistic movement powered only by nerves.

Warren sighed in relief. First he was relieved not to have been snake bitten and secondly he was relieved not to have been shot.

Thomas then looked at the suffering deer and discharged the remaining shell inside the double barreled sixteen gauge shotgun. It was the right thing to do and Warren was proud of him.

"Someone had shot him and didn't kill 'em," Warren said to Thomas.

"I know," the boy replied as the men looked at the lifeless buck with small antlers protruding from it's head.

Warren walked back to the truck and returned with a pearl handled filet knife. He then cut the buck's throat to drain the blood in effort of keeping the meat untainted.

"Let's drag 'em to the truck," Warren said as Thomas reached for the deer's hind legs.

"We going to butcher the buck?" Thomas asked curiously.

"He needs butchering right away," Warren explained. "Let's take 'em on down to Jug Island. I know a fellow that'll do it for us while we talk to the other fellow about the fish nets."

Warren found his nephew quite agreeable with the idea. The two carried on with their plans. An old Florida Cracker named Ethan Belle skinned and butchered the buck while Warren and the other gentleman discussed the fishing nets.

While Warren spoke with the gruff looking character, he couldn't help but notice Thomas being captivated by a small row boat. The craft's width was nearly in excess of it's length. The hull was white and the battleship gray trim added the finishing touches to give the little boat added charisma. It was an appealing little vessel that could be easily handled on the Suwannee River, at Dead Man's Bay, or even in New England. It was however very unlikely the lad would be going to New England. Just the same, the little boat possessed the charm to mingle among fancier vessels anywhere.

As Warren and the gentleman continued to talk, Sir Thomas sauntered back to the panel truck where he patiently awaited his uncle to conclude business. At last, business was concluded and Warren proceeded to the panel truck.

"You didn't buy the nets?" Thomas asked.

"Yea I bought them," Warren replied. "The fellow's going to bring them up a little later. He has to get them ready and repair a place or two in them."

"We going after the deer?" Thomas then probed.

Warren pulled his watch from his pocket and glanced at it. He then looked up into the sky and finally looked over at Thomas.

"Let's give Ethan a little more time," Warren said. "Why don't I buy you a cup of coffee down at the store?"

"That'll work," replied Thomas with his genuine grin taking back over.

The store was called just that, The Store. It was a sprawling building of board and batten with a rusted tin roof. A large porch extended across the front of it and on the porch were many rocking chairs. A few of the chairs were occupied by some rough, craggy looking characters. Incidentally, they were passing back and forth a jug of homemade liquor.

To say the least, Thomas was almost uncomfortable around such characters but proceeded inside behind Warren.

"Afternoon, Mr. McKinley," one of the men said.

"Good to see you, Mr. Mac," another commented.

"Fine looking young man you got there with you," a third man stated. "I bet that's one of Rose's."

Thomas shook the man's hand and introduced himself.

"You know my ma?" The young man asked.

"Oh I know all your family son," the man replied. "The McKinley's been comin' down here for years."

"That boat kicker over there in the trough," Warren said as he pointed to it, "you aiming to sell it, Drew?"

"I bought that old thing from an old widow woman the other day and got it running. Yea I reckon I'll sell," Thomas' new found acquaintance said.

"How much?" Warren asked.

"Well," the man mumbled in thought. "Don't I owe you ten dollars, Warren?"

"Seems like it," Warren replied.

"Ten Dollars," the man quickly said with a grin.

"I'll get it on my way out," replied Warren.

At last, Thomas and Warren were seated inside the store. A homely looking waitress automatically carried Warren a cup of black coffee and asked Thomas what he would like. She soon returned with a duplicate of Warren's unspoken order.

Quietly Thomas and his uncle sipped their black coffee as they observed two old codgers playing checkers. The large window allowed plenty of sunlight to infiltrate the dusty room. It also told on the maid service for the spider webs were obvious. Of course the maid service was non existing.

"Thomas," Warren began, "I'm awful proud of that shot you made on our way up here."

"I'm sorry about dragging around gettin' there," Thomas then said. "If you'd have gotten snake bit I would have felt awful bad."

"Well," Warren said with his understanding smile, "sometimes you just have to trust me, Thomas."

That was a reality check for Thomas. He could not trust Warren McKinley knowing what he knew about his conversation with Pierce. There again, he had just as soon trust Warren as he had Porter. Nonetheless, Thomas regained his senses and renewed his skepticism within concerning Warren McKinley.

"What are you going to do with the kicker?" Thomas asked.

"There is a fellow back at the bay that has been looking for one," Warren explained. "I'll sell it to him for fifteen dollars."

After loading the boat kicker, the traveling duo returned to Ethan Belle's and picked up their portion of the deer meat. Ethan was given a smart amount of the venison for having butchered it. After doing so, Dead Man's Bay was their destination.

Chapter XVI

Supper time made it's way into Dead Man's Bay. The McKinley household was seated around a supper table filled with venison, grits, biscuits, cane syrup, and collard greens.

"Thomas put the meat on the table tonight," Warren boasted.

"I still can't believe he made that shot," Rose commented. "You say the deer was running fast?"

"Oh yes," Warren confirmed as he winked at Thomas. "He was in a full speed run."

James McKinley caught a glimpse of the wink and then looked at Thomas quite seriously.

"Did you have to lead him with your aim, Thomas?" James asked.

"Well," replied the lad in attempt to fib. "I might have led him just a little bit. Why do you ask, Grandpa?"

"Oh just wondering," answered James McKinley with a slight smile. "I think I killed a deer like that one time my own self."

Allen Wheeler listened attentively as the others talked of Thomas killing the buck. It was all rather important to him. He wanted complete knowledge of each and every little detail.

"Now my daddy," Allen finally began rather boastfully. "He can really kill deer."

Thomas noticed his mother's unusual reaction to Allen's comment. He also noticed the way his grandmother looked at her when Allen made the statement.

Rose then gracefully excused herself with Martha McKinley following behind her. There Thomas Wheeler set feeling saddened. He felt enough sadness in the fact his father was obviously missing in action but to compound matters, he felt a heavier burden due to the fact his mother was apparently so disturbed.

"How you like the boat Allen?" Thomas asked.

"It's a good boat," the little fellow replied. "One day I'll have a real boat just like it and me and you and Papa and Grandpa McKinley and Ma and Grandma and everybody can go on the gulf in it."

"Sure you will," replied Thomas with a smile as James, Warren, and Melanie looked on with their own smiles of contentment.

Warren then leaned back in his chair as he sipped a cup of coffee while gazing over at Melanie.

"Think I should ask him?" Warren asked of Melanie.

"Now is as good a time as any I suppose," she replied with a consenting grin.

"Thomas Wheeler," Warren dandily announced, "would you accompany me over to the fish house to look at the nets?"

Reluctantly the lad agreed. As they walked outside and over to the fish house, Thomas thought it to be unusual that Melanie and his grandfather were following.

"Well look a here," Amos called from behind the metal fish house. "Looks like somebody left a mighty fine little boat."

"What do you think?" Warren asked Thomas as they all admired the little gray and white boat. The kicker Warren purchased in Jug Island had also been mounted on the back of the little boat.

"Pretty sharp," Thomas said approvingly.

"She's all yours," Warren said.

"Mine?" Thomas asked in shock. "But Uncle Warren...."

"No buts," Warren replied. "It's a gift from me to you."

Thomas stood in astonishment. He had truly became a torn young man. He so badly wanted to accept the boat but was skeptical of accepting a gift from someone he was spying on. The lad then looked at Amos, Melanie, and his grandfather. He knew he had to accept the boat for their sake. It would be unfair to them to be openly rude to Warren, he thought.

"Thank you, Warren," the young man said. "I'll take good care of it."

"I know you will, Thomas," Warren so proudly commented. "That is why I wanted to do this for you."

"It is approaching dark now," James advised. "Why don't we all get a good night's sleep and make Thomas give us all a ride in the morning?"

James McKinley and Melanie meandered back to the large bungalow. Thomas accompanied his old pal Amos to his quarters and Warren had to go check some fish traps. As for the appealing little boat, it remained tied to the dock directly behind the fish house.

As Amos and Thomas strolled past the office door of the Bay Fish Camp, Thomas couldn't help noticing the door being unlocked. Locked doors were very unusual in Dead Man's Bay but Warren insisted upon keeping his office door locked when he was not there.

After a very brief visit with Amos, Thomas started back to the bungalow of his grandparents. When he approached the unlocked and slightly ajar office door, he found himself unable to resist the temptation of having a look inside.

The office was approximately eight feet in width and twenty feet in length. Warren's desk sat in the back and faced the door. There was a table with four straight chairs near the entrance and filing cabinets stood along a long wall. The other wall had two book shelves with a good variety of reading material.

Checking closely for onlookers, Thomas opened the file drawer labeled "P." Just as he figured, there was a single file for Pierce. It was not Scott Pierce. Instead, it was Sam Pierce.

The file only contained small books with numbers written in them. Most of the numbers were four digit and beside them were peoples' names. The young man also found it interesting that every few pages in each book were dated.

Thomas thought what he found to be very interesting. He deemed it interesting enough he planned to notify Jack of his findings. As he slowly and gently replaced the files and easily stepped toward the door, he saw Warren walking toward the office.

"Hey, Warren," Thomas called out as he exited the small office. "I figured somebody should lock the door."

"That's O.K., Thomas," Warren replied. "I have to go back in there for a while."

"Alright," Thomas replied as he began to saunter away.

Warren pulled a pad from his coat that was exactly as those Thomas had found in the files of one Sam Pierce. Just as Thomas turned around to glance back at his uncle, he observed Warren opening the filing cabinet drawer labeled "P."

Just then Thomas heard his mother call for him from the large bungalow.

"Thomas Wheeler," she yelled out.

"Yea, Ma," the lad called back.

"Thomas, it's been a long day and morning will be here before you know it. Why don't you come on in?"

"I know, I know," Thomas Wheeler replied in a tone that only he could hear. "I gotta wake the chickens in the morning and tell 'em to start laying."

"Thomas!" Rose called again.

"I'm on my way now, Ma," the lad answered.

Thomas entered the kitchen and found his mother setting alone over a cup of coffee. She appeared weary as she slowly sipped the coffee and nibbled on a piece of biscuit left over from supper.

"Have a cup of coffee?" Rose asked Thomas.

"Believe I will," her son replied.

Thomas pulled down a cup and poured himself some black coffee. He then sat down at the table across from his mother without doctoring his cup of java.

"Any word from Pa?" Thomas asked.

"No, Thomas," she replied. "There is no word as of yet. I think we should have heard something by now though," she confirmed.

"I believe you are right," the young man replied in a hopeless tone.

It was the first time that Rose and Thomas had openly considered the worst in Charles Wheeler's fate. Thomas then turned his attention to the roomy kitchen. It was a typical cracker kitchen.

"Thomas," Rose said in a voice that lacked the strength of her normal tone, "I want to see your boat."

She then smiled as the young man's attention turned from worry of his father's well being.

"You want to see it now?" Thomas asked.

"I sure do," she said with a smile.

The mother and son finished their coffee and meandered down to the river bank where the small craft sashayed atop the rippling river.

"Oh, it's a fine little boat," Rose commented. "What are you going to call it?" She then asked.

"I hadn't really thought about naming it," Thomas replied. "What do you think I should call it?"

Rose appeared in deep thought as she peered at the little vessel. She walked back and forth inspecting it's seaworthiness. At last she looked at her son and gently smiled.

"In Dead Man's Bay a young man's first boat is usually something very special," she said. "I think you should name the boat *Cracker Princess.*"

"Can you paint that on there?" Thomas asked.

"If we can round up some paint," Rose reluctantly replied.

"Thanks, Ma," Thomas genuinely replied. "Ma, I have to go check on Amos."

"I know," Rose said. "Don't be too late getting to sleep."

"O.K., Ma," said a smiling Thomas.

Rose returned to the bungalow to turn in for the evening. She would write Charles a letter in hopes of him receiving it. She was however skeptical of his ever reading it. Nonetheless she had to write him whether he received it or not. Thinking of how much she loved him and how much the children needed to know him, she wrote with tears.

Dearest Charles,

I do hope you receive this letter. We are all so terribly worried about you for it has now been five months since we last heard anything from you. I have come down to the bay for a few days with the kids. Nancy is really becoming a little southern lady. She constantly wants to know when her papa is coming home. Allen is growing like a weed. Charles, I think he's going to be a carpenter as much as he likes to hammer. As for Thomas, well he is a little man now. He spends most of his time taking care of the farming.

He thinks I don't know it but he has made some extra money breaking the Captain's horses. I feel terrible for allowing it to go on but he is quite a determined young man. As far as everything else goes, things are pretty normal. My mother and father are in good health. Melanie is just wonderful Charles. I so enjoy her company. Warren is still Warren. He tries so very hard to please everyone. He is so insistent that he sends me forty dollars each month while you are away. I cannot find it in my heart to let Thomas know because he feels that he should be the one to provide for us while you are gone. I do not want to destroy his self-esteem. Only Warren, Melanie, and I have shared this secret. Jack is still in Suwannee County doing whatever it is Jack does and Stella is still in Chatahoochee. Hopefully the poor dear will be able to find happiness someday.

I think of you always and shall cherish the day we reunite.

Love,
Rose

Rose Wheeler soon dozed off into sleep as a peaceful Steinhachee River passed the McKinley's by.

As for Thomas, he and Amos discussed their own plans of farm life once they return to Suwannee County.

"Amos," Thomas finally probed. "What would a fellow have some books with numbers, names, and dates in them for?"

"Who has books like that?" Amos quickly asked.

"Just answer me, Amos," Thomas pleaded.

"Your Uncle Warren is a numbers man," Amos openly admitted.

"How you know I was talking about Warren?" Thomas then asked.

Amos smiled as he began packing his corncob pipe for a fragrant smoke of the special blend pipe tobacco he occasionally enjoyed. He carefully measured his tobacco in the bowl of the pipe prior to packing it. As Amos lit his pipe, he cut his eyes and looked at his young protege.

"Funny thing is," Amos began, "your Uncle Jack, he be a numbers man too. I bet you didn't know that either did you?"

"No I didn't," Thomas admitted.

"That's a fact," confirmed Amos.

Thomas had a reasonable knowledge of the numbers business. He was unsure how it worked exactly but realized it was illegal. The part he was unclear of was how both of his uncles could be involved in the same thing and dislike one another so.

"Are they involved in the same racket?" Thomas asked genuinely.

"Oh no," Amos replied gently. "Jack is just a little numbers man around. Just for fun mainly. He might makes a little money with it but not much. I thinks Zeb's mainly behind that."

"And Warren?" Thomas asked.

"Warren," Amos chuckled as he drew from his pipe. "Now Warren, that's a different story there all together. He's in it for the bigs money. I hear tell his numbers comes from the islands you know. He may be a big man here on the gulf but he's probably a little man in a big outfit."

"Grandpa McKinley involved?" Thomas then asked in a very serious tone.

"Oh no," Amos replied. "Your Grandpa would never get into anything like that he's too good of a man. I believe he knows about Jack and Warren but he ain't in the numbers game."

"How did they both get into the same type of thing?" Thomas asked.

"The company they keep," Amos replied with a slight grin. "Now don't go tellin' anybody Old Amos been tellin' you about the shortcoming of the McKinley Brothers 'cause it ain't none of my business."

For a short while Thomas and Amos sat in total silence. It was rare for Thomas to hear Amos in such an information sharing mood and was sure his mentor would clam up any given moment. Therefore, he thought diligently of any questions he thought needed asking.

Thomas was aware that Amos knew much of what went on in North Florida. For many years, Amos had played a lackadaisical character that cared less of what happened around him. All the while, he was busy listening and observing. That was the two qualities he had so tried to instill into his young friend.

"Who do you think is behind Warren in the numbers racket?" Thomas asked.

"I ain't all that sure 'bout that," Amos admitted.

Thomas asked no more questions. Amos more than likely did not know who Warren reported to. The young man however felt sure he knew. Sam Pierce was undoubtedly the numbers man above Warren McKinley.

Chapter XVII

A fall rain had set in over Suwannee County. It followed the river's bed right through the Suwannee Valley Area. As the fall's early morning rain came, Zeb was awakened by the rolling thunder. Zeb often took a little nap after closing The Club Palmetto down. When he awoke that morning, he pulled his pocket watch and held it next to the kerosene lamp. Realizing it was already 5:00 a.m., Zeb sauntered over and stood with the door slightly ajar so that he could enjoy such a peaceful scene. The annual changing of the leaves about the various trees was truly accented by the soft descent of small drops of precipitation onto their stems and leaves of gold. The lightening provided ample lighting to enhance the scene.

As Zeb looked at a spider web that glistened in the morning rain, he savored its beauty. Amazing, he thought. Another natural thing that could be so beautiful in a cleansing rain or so ugly when one mistakenly walks into it. He then found comfort in listening to the gentle pressing of the rain about the river woods. It was a sound that seemed to stand guard against outside disturbances. Things are however not always what they seem.

The trampling of human beings through the woods alarmed Zeb. He first heard one faint voice and then there was another and then another. At last three men holding umbrellas walked up to the front door where he stood. It was unusual to see men carrying umbrellas in that neck of the woods. Of course, these were three out of place looking characters anyway.

"We're here to look at your place," said the one in the center.

It was evident he was in charge. He was the one in the finest suit of clothes. It was a dark pinstriped suit. The white fedora on his head was cocked just a little to the side thus portraying an abundance of self-confidence.

As for the other two, Zeb had seen their type all over the States. They were just a couple of overfed bullies on somebody's payroll to protect the loudmouth in the center. That didn't really impress Zeb. He didn't see the presence of a musical ability in any of the three.

"Well you see it," Zeb replied as he stepped out through the front door and closed it behind him. "Is there any particular reason you want to look at my place?"

"Well it is customary, sir, that a fellow looks a place over before buying it," said the center man in the white fedora.

"Well I ain't in the market to sell," Zeb said. "So if you gentlemen will be so kind as to leave, I'll just get back to my........"

"Allow me to introduce myself," the man in the fedora interrupted. "I am Scott Pierce, son of Sam Pierce. Now surely you have heard of my father."

"Come in," Zeb reluctantly said.

Pierce and his goons stepped in out of the weather and rudely dropped their hats and coats on a couple of tables. Scott Pierce then looked about the placed and flashed a ghastly grin.

"I like it," he said in his distinctive voice. He wasn't a loud talker and sounded as if he were talking through his nose. "Yeah, I can turn this joint into something real good."

Pierce's sidekicks walked around the tiny establishment and observed the photographs that graced the walls. Zeb remained quite as he sipped a cup of coffee.

"Fix me a drink boys," Pierce said.

"Ah kinda early ain't it, Boss?" One of them replied.

"Fix me a drink I told you!" Pierce exclaimed.

He then looked at the calm Zeb and began to chuckle as he inspected his untarnished, manicured fingernails.

"They're good employees but I have to put them in their place from time to time. Speaking of employees, I plan to keep you on after I take over here," advised Pierce.

"Yea but it just ain't that easy you see," Zeb began to explain. "I have a partner here and I don't know if he's willing to sell or not."

"Oh he'll be willing to O.K.," Pierce replied.

Pierce had no knowledge Zeb's silent partner was Jack McKinley. The same Jack McKinley that had called Pierce out and was presently anticipating a confrontation with him.

"Your partner around?" The lunatic anxiously inquired.

"Naw, sir, he ain't," Zeb answered.

"They didn't tell me about you having a partner," Pierce muttered. "What is his name?"

"McKinley," Zeb replied, "a fellow by the name of Jack McKinley. You heard of 'em?"

Pierce looked very angry to say the least. It seemed to him that the McKinley's had been a thorn in his side for too long. He was ready to put a stop to it once and for all. He took a gulp of the glass of whisky that had just been sat before him and then wiped his mouth with the back of his hand.

"This Jack McKinley," he began, "what is he some kind of local hero? I hear he thinks he's pretty tough. Is he?"

"McKinley ain't nothin'," Zeb replied. "Loudmouth, always been a loudmouth."

Pierce looked at Zeb and grinned largely. He then instructed his goons to go for a walk and refilled his glass with crystal clear home-made whiskey. After doing so, Pierce sat down at the table directly across from Zeb.

"You talk like you don't like McKinley," suggested Pierce.

"I don't. Never did," replied Zeb solemnly.

"So why are you two in business together?" Pierce probed.

"I've been trying to get his half since we built. So far he ain't gave in," Zeb explained.

Again, Pierce smiled at Zeb. Undoubtedly, the devious madman had a plan at hand.

"Mind if I call you Zeb?" Pierce asked.

"Not at all," replied Zeb with a cordial smile.

"Well, Zeb," Pierce began, "you gonna make twice the dough with me than what you did with McKinley."

"You think you can make 'em sell?" Zeb asked.

"I can make that sod buster do what ever I want him to," Pierce replied in a sarcastic tone. "I'll talk to him today. I understand he's at his sister's place. He sent word to me he wants to see me. Talks like he's calling me out," Pierce explained.

"No need to worry," Zeb easily replied. "He ain't nothin' but a sot drunk. Why don't you show up around four o'clock this afternoon and he'll give you whatever you want for a bottle of whiskey."

"And if something was to happen to him," Pierce chuckled. "Oh well it just happens."

The two men sat and talked for a few minutes while the two side-kicks of Pierce stood outside in the cold. Pierce explained to Zeb his plans of giving The Club Palmetto a more modern appeal. He also emphasized his intent of changing the club's clientele to the more ritzy.

At last, Pierce informed Zeb of his gambling ideas for The Club Palmetto. Without Zeb even telling him, Pierce was already aware he had been pushing numbers through the Club Palmetto. However, Scott Pierce told Zeb they were going for bigger and better things.

"Well I guess I see McKinley from here," Pierce said as he stood to leave. "I've been needing to see the bum anyway."

"It's like I said," Zeb reminded him. "It'll be best to see him around four this afternoon. That'll give him just the right time to get tanked up."

"You can go ahead and start cleaning this place," Pierce demanded as he walked out into the crisp, damp atmosphere.

That was a bit insulting to Zeb. The Club Palmetto was not big nor was it very modern but Zeb kept it neat and clean. But nonetheless he agreed with Scott Pierce and then watched him vanish into the woods.

Zeb waited for about thirty minutes. When the rain had ceased, he rushed down to his little boat on the river. Zeb pulled the rope and fired up the small kicker and headed half a mile up river and saw Mut Jacobson. Mut's house would have been more fitting for a child's fort. It was just one small room of sawmill slabs wedged in between two trees on the bank of the river.

"You in there, Mut?" Zeb called. "Hey, Mut."

Mut came outside yawning and stretching. Trying to focus on who had interrupted his peaceful slumber.

"That you, Zeb?" Asked Mut in his deep, gruff voice.

"Yea it's me," Zeb replied. "I need you to go to Charles Wheeler's place and tell Jack McKinley to meet me at Charles Springs quick. I'll explain later."

"Why?" the confused Mut asked.

"I'll explain later," Zeb said. "But please, Mut, hurry it up."

Zeb then cranked his small kicker back up and was gone.

Chapter XVIII

Mut Jacobson somehow came to life after a night of fishing and walked to the Wheeler home to give Jack McKinley a message. It was a four mile walk so Mut was able to make it in about ninety minutes. Although the river rat was tempted to sidetrack his path at various points, he remained true to Zeb's instructions.

This is gonna cost Old Zeb a whole night of free drinkin', Mut thought to himself. He then laughed aloud as he picked up a broken branch from the road side and began whittling as he walked.

"If he were to give me a free night of drinkin', this'll be an expensive favor," Mut said to himself and a hidden covey of quail.

As Jack McKinley was replacing a busted slat on the makeshift corral outside the small animal barn, he spotted Mut coming up the road. In keeping with tradition of being neighborly, Jack had Mut and himself each a cup of coffee poured by the time Mut reached him.

"Mut Jacobson," Jack called out, "what in the world brings you here on such a fine wet morning old friend?"

"Two tired feet," Mut replied in laughter.

"Well then," Jack said, "have a cup of coffee and set a spell."

Mut thanked Jack and took the coffee. The two men casually sipped the coffee as Jack told Mut about the work he had been doing on his sister's place.

"Zeb sent me here," Mut finally said.

"Zeb?" Jack replied rhetorically. "Anything wrong?"

"He didn't say," explained Mut. "Jack, he needs to meet with you at Charles Springs in a hurry."

"Where you headed?" Jack asked.

"Suppose I'll hoof it on back to the shack," Mut said.

"Jump in the truck and I'll drop you off," instructed Jack McKinley as he engaged in a brisk walk to the Chevrolet truck.

Jack drove quickly to Mut's shack and again thanked Mut for carrying him word of Zeb's request for a meeting. Jack knew something wasn't just right or Zeb would have come himself. He also knew a meeting at Charles Springs was unusual instead of The Club Palmetto.

After Mut got out of the truck, Jack pulled back his coat and pulled from a shoulder holster a .45 caliber revolver. It was a beautiful gun that had been manufactured by Sam Colt. The barrel was six inches in length and the handle was of pearl.

Jack liked Mut and had always liked him. He was however aware of Mut's capability to engage in less than honorable activity. In all honesty, Jack was skeptical of his upcoming rendezvous being with Zeb. After insuring the revolver held six rounds of ammunition, Jack drove cautiously to Charles Springs.

Charles Springs was a special place to Jack. He had spent many days and nights there. It was there he spent much of his adolescent years escaping the pains of a school room. Later in life, it was often Charles Springs that had cast a tranquil incantation upon Jack and his bride, Stella.

At first, Jack considered driving up to the springs but changed his mind and left the truck parked off into the woods about a quarter mile away. He figured by doing so, he could surprise those awaiting him rather than allowing them to surprise him. As he quietly ambled through the river woods, Zeb peacefully awaited him.

Jack was a skilled woods traveler to say the least. Of course, he had spent virtually all his life rambling the woodlands of North Florida. Instead of walking right up to the spring, he circled around about three hundred feet downstream the river. Quietly, he marched up stream along the river bank. He then followed the cold, pure water back to the spring where Zeb sat upon the natural rock bridge.

For a moment, Jack observed Zeb and the surroundings. He then quietly slipped up behind his unsuspecting friend.

"You looking for me?" Jack asked from behind Zeb.

Needless to say, Zeb jumped from surprise.

"Jack!" Zeb shouted in surprise and maybe a touch of fright. "Ain't nary bit of since in you doin' that to me."

Laughter overcame Jack McKinley as he peered at his frightened friend. Zeb was not laughing however. He had a serious look about his face thus causing Jack's laughter to be cut short.

"What's wrong Zeb?" Jack asked.

"Does the name Scott Pierce mean anything to you?" responded Zeb.

"Yea, trouble," replied Jack in a sadistic manner as his facial expression became hard and irritated.

"Well, he came to the club," Zeb informed Jack.

"How dare he set foot in our establishment. When did that hooligan go there?" Jack probed.

"Just this mornin'," Zeb explained. He then went into detail of their whole conversation leaving out no details. "Jack, he's goin' to see you at four this afternoon and he's up to no good, Jack."

After recollecting his thoughts and composure, Jack replied. "I don't really see anything to be concerned about. Let 'em come."

"Don't be a fool Jack," warned Zeb. "He's aimin' to kill you."

Jack then removed his coat and sat down on the rock bridge beside Zeb. For a moment the two men were quiet as they listened to the water boil from the ground and flow in it's continuous journey to the Gulf of Mexico.

"Surely you do not believe Pierce can take me?" Jack asked Zeb.

"No, I don't," Zeb reluctantly replied. "Jack, I just think he don't need to get the chance."

"Well I don't think he has much of a chance," Jack replied with a smile. "It looks to me like you set the old boy up pretty good."

"What is his thinkin'?" Zeb asked Jack.

"The bum's still sore at my brother-in-law for testifying against him about the theft ring he had. I reckon he figures if he can get rid of my sister's family he can do pretty well what he wants without people seeing what's going on," Jack explained. "You know, I think he's just that low down mean, too."

"That old boy's plum deranged," commented Zeb. "An' you know it too, Jack."

"Yep," Jack replied as he lit a Lucky Strike, "he's deranged alright."

"You think he really wants to buy the club?" Zeb then asked.

"Oh, yea," Jack said. "It would be the perfect little gamblin' hole for him and his big city cronies to meet. I can't speak for you Zeb but I ain't a sellin'."

Zeb grinned from ear to ear. That's what he knew Jack would say and that's all he wanted to hear.

"I ain't a aimin' to sell neither," commented Zeb. "And we's a gonna tell Pierce just that this afternoon."

"No, we ain't!" Jack replied.

"What do you mean?" retorted Zeb.

"I mean we ain't," Jack stated. "I am. You ain't gonna be there."

"An' just why not?" Zeb demanded.

"This is my battle. I'll handle it," explained Jack. "You need to make sure things run as they should at the club."

Zeb knew Jack was right about being at the club but felt the battle was equally his to fight.

"Zeb," Jack began to explain, "this Pierce thing runs deeper than just The Club Palmetto. Of course you know about my brother losing the place to his pa in a poker game,"

"I know," Zeb commented.

"But now he's been threatening my sister and her children because of Charles testifying against him in court," Jack further explained. "You know, Zeb, my family ain't close like we used to be and I reckon that's mostly my fault. But I be blessed if I'm going to stand still for a sorry soul like Scott Pierce to push any one of them around."

Zeb had spent many hours with Jack McKinley over the years. Some of them had been happy others tense, and yet many of the hours had been sad ones. At that moment however, was the first time Zeb had seen Jack literally cry. Once the tears began, they didn't stop so soon. In silence, the two men sat on that rock bridge.

"Well, looks like the rain's all gone and it's gonna be a pretty day or two," Zeb finally commented.

"Those are the prettiest little children Rose has you could ever lay eyes on. They are plenty smart too, Zeb," Jack sadly boasted.

"I'm sure they is," Zeb answered.

"That Thomas," Jack softly began with a hint of a smile. "You know Zeb, he's a lot like his Old Uncle Jack."

"Lawd help the child," Zeb replied in attempt to lighten the conversation.

"You know, he thinks I need to go and talk with Stella," Jack said.

"Maybe he's just a touch smarter than his Old Uncle Jack," Zeb replied in a continued effort of adding humor.

Although Thomas had never told Jack he should go talk to Stella, maybe Jack was right. Maybe the lad had tried telling him to do so. Furthermore, Jack knew within his own heart it should be done.

"So you told Pierce to catch me around four this afternoon?" Jack asked in confirmation.

"I did," Zeb replied.

"You told 'em I'd be feeling no pain did ya," Jack further probed.

"I did," Zeb confirmed.

"Looks like my foe, Mr. Pierce just might be a little disappointed," commented Jack.

"That's why I sent after ya," replied his trusted friend.

As the two men stood in preparation to depart Charles Springs, Zeb noticed his old friend no longer got up as quickly as he once might have. Zeb did not figure Jack to be any less capable than ever before but was concerned that he might have slowed considerably where altercations were concerned.

"Jack," Zeb said in a very serious tone.

"Yes, Zeb," Jack replied.

"I just want you to be real careful, Jack," Zeb said. "Pierce ain't got no sense."

Jack never replied. He appreciated what Zeb had to say but he didn't really want to talk about the inescapable showdown that lay ahead.

"How did you get here?" Jack asked.

"Walked," replied Zeb.

"Want a ride?" Jack asked.

"Better not," Zeb said, "Pierce might see us. We don't want him thinkin' I went and told you now do we?"

The two men went their opposite directions. Zeb returned to The Club Palmetto and Jack journeyed back to the Wheeler place.

As Zeb walked along the dirt road that led up to The Club Palmetto, he saw a fellow coming down the road who was also on foot. He was an unusual character indeed. His hair was dark and not groomed. The stranger wore a beard and a patch over his left eye and his left arm was missing. In it's place was a hook.

As the two men neared one another, the stranger turned into the woods in effort to avoid contact with Zeb. Apparently he hid well for Zeb was unable to see him in the thicket as he walked by.

Chapter XIX

As Zeb returned to The Club Palmetto from his Charles Springs meeting with Jack, his concerns intensified. He could see no single mortal outmatching his friend, McKinley. However, he realized Jack would not be facing only one man.

It was10:00 a.m. and time was running out. Zeb knew what he had to do and also realized it would very much anger Jack. Zeb was aware of Warren McKinley's connection with Sam Pierce and further realized Sam Pierce was the only person that could control his son, Scott.

After a short time of consideration, Zeb walked up river a short piece where he had a small cracker house. The house wasn't much at all. It had all the things he needed though. There he had a relatively dry closet for his fop clothing, an outhouse, a wood burning stove, and a bed in a dry spot. It was however always tidy and in order as Zeb had a lady friend that would ensure that.

Out back was a thirty-eight Ford coupe he had used more than once to transport bootlegged whiskey. As Zeb walked up to the coupe he rubbed her hood gently and said, "Please baby if you's ever started up for Old Zeb, start up now."

He fiddled around with the carburetor for a little while and crossed his left fingers as he turned the makeshift ignition. The little coupe fired up and Zeb drove at a high rate of speed all the way to Mayo.

In Mayo, he made a very brief stop to get gas. While there, he purchased an R.C. Cola and a Moon Pie and was on his way to Dead Man's Bay. As Zeb encountered the sand ruts on the road to the Bay, he never slowed. Often he would almost lose control of the car but somehow managed to keep her on all fours. He had little time to get word to Warren McKinley of the brewing troubles in Suwannee County. He just hoped Warren would be there.

Zeb knew where the Bay Fish Camp was for he and Jack had been there on previous occasions. In more pleasant days, Zeb would accompany Jack McKinley on cattle drives that would often carry them near the Bay. In earlier years, the McKinley family owned scrub cows in the woods surrounding Dead Man's Bay in addition to their Suwannee County herds.

By the time Zeb reached the Bay, he was unsure if his car would ever travel again as it was running extremely hot. Rusty water poured from the tattered radiator. Nonetheless, he had made his destination.

Zeb was a God fearing sinner who realized once again the Good Lord was on his side when his car completely died less than one hundred yards from the camp. He allowed the car to roll to a stop on the road's side and quickly ran to the office of Warren McKinley. As luck would have it, Warren was inside the office.

Zeb was a little short of breath when he abruptly entered the office of Warren McKinley and looked at him.

"Zeb!" Exclaimed an alarmed Warren. "What on earth brings you here?"

"Jack's in trouble, Warren," Zeb said. "Please, Warren, you've gotta help."

"What kind of trouble?" A cautious Warren asked. "Is Jack O.K.?"

"He's got real trouble headed his way, Warren," Zeb announced. "You're probably the only person that can help 'em."

Zeb explained the ordeal to Warren of Scott Pierce. He began with the troubles of Pierce and Rose's family and led up to Pierce's intent of seeing Jack later that very day. As Zeb spoke, Warren listened attentively.

"We cannot allow this meeting with Jack and Pierce," Warren advised. "How receptive do you think Jack will be to my help though?"

"That don't matter," Zeb quickly replied. "Especially if you got yourself a plan we can use."

"To begin with," Warren commented, "time is of an essence. We have under five hours until four o'clock. What I would like for you to do Zeb is go to Scott Pierce as fast as possible and detain him from going to Jack as long as you possibly can. Speak of your plans to take care of the club once Jack is out of the way."

"How will I get back?" Zeb asked.

"Don't worry about that," Warren advised. "I will get you back to Suwannee County rather quickly."

"Let's go," Zeb commented with a concerned look in his eye.

"I must first prepare myself," Warren advised. "You must be hungry. Can I offer you a quick bite of dinner?"

Warren McKinley was indeed a gentleman of etiquette. He did however get it honest. James McKinley was a true gentleman and Miss Martha was a very gracious lady.

Although they could all muster up the social graces to rub elbows with Great Britain's finest, the McKinley's would always refer to the evening meal as supper and the noon meal as dinner. That was just the

North Florida Cracker way and they were genuine North Florida Crackers.

"No thank you," Zeb replied. "I'm just not all that hungry, Mr. Warren."

"Very well," Warren said, "if you will excuse me a moment, I will need to change my attire."

Warren briskly walked to the small cottage he and Melanie occupied. Zeb stepped outside the office to await Warren's return. As Zeb lit a cigarette, he gazed about the compound of the Bay Fish Camp trying to occupy his troubled mind with something other than Scott Pierce.

Inside the cabin, Warren took off his dress shoes and pinstriped suit. He then slipped into a pair of khaki pants. He kept the white shirt on and over it, he put on a field vest. The vest had a total of eighteen pockets. In fact, there were pockets inside some of the pockets of the vest. Warren then put on a pair of worn brogans. Finally, he placed an older brown fedora upon his head and slightly tilted it to the right.

Just over the right front pocket of Warren's vest, he placed a derringer into a hidden pocket. He then placed a gun belt around the lengthy vest and fastened it. Upon fastening the gun belt, Warren slipped a .45 caliber colt revolver into the holster. At last, he dropped a handful of .45 rounds into one of the vest's pockets.

He then looked about the homespun cottage and sighed as he walked out. Outside, Warren lit a Lucky Strike cigarette and looked toward the large bungalow of his parents. There was nobody there. Martha, Rose, Melanie, Allen, and Nancy were all at the Church. Some of the local ladies and children had gathered that day for a good general cleaning of the Primitive Baptist Church.

As for Thomas and Amos, they were enjoying the gulf air aboard the "Cracker Princess". In their opinion, she was the finest vessel in the gulf. James McKinley was down at the little cafe enjoying a cup of coffee with a few old friends.

Zeb stood ready to go as Warren hastily walked back toward the office. Zeb noted the sudden change in Warren McKinley's appearance. He had never pictured Warren dressing in such a manner but was somewhat impressed with McKinley's appearance of intent to standup to Pierce.

"You got a plan?" Zeb asked.

"No," Warren readily replied. "You ready?"

"Yes sir," Zeb said. "How we goin'?"

"Let's take the panel truck," Warren said as he pointed to the black Chevrolet panel truck used by the fish camp. "Go on over there and I'll be right behind you."

Warren then walked inside the fish house where eight men worked diligently at cleaning fish. He called the attention of Blue Thompson.

Blue had been working for McKinley's family since the grandfather ran the operation. Over the years, Blue had been left in charge of the entire operation when duty called the family elsewhere.

"Blue," Warren said as Thompson looked at him rather awkwardly, "I have to go away for a while on business. You'll have to be in charge. Tell Pa I don't know when I'll be back."

"Where you going?" Blue asked of Warren.

"It doesn't matter Blue," Warren replied. "Now you take care of things. Especially my family. You should find ample operating funds if needed in the file cabinet furthest from the door. It is in the back of the second file cabinet drawer in a cigar box."

Warren and Zeb then got into the panel truck and drove up river a short piece with no conversation. Zeb had readied himself for the lengthy ride and appeared confused when Warren pulled off the road and through a tree line. On the other side of the tree line was a quarter mile strip of grass among the palm trees. At the end of the grass strip was a yellow airplane.

Warren quickly drove the panel truck to the airplane, got out and hurriedly conducted a pre-flight inspection.

"Get in," Warren instructed Zeb.

"Oh, naw sir," the black gentleman candidly replied while definitely shaking his head back and forth. "I don't ride in those things, naw sir."

Warren got inside the cockpit and then got back out. He then grabbed the propeller and pulled down on it. The plane cranked and again he looked over at Zeb.

"Get in," Warren said in an authoritative voice.

"I think I made myself clear," Zeb yelled over the roar of the sixty-five horsepower Continental engine. "I don't fly!"

"You do now!" Warren yelled back as he drew his revolver and pointed it at Zeb's Torso. "Now get in."

"Oh, yes sir," Zeb replied as he quickly climbed into the passenger's seat of the L-4 Piper Cub.

Warren then re-holstered his revolver and climbed into the plane. In just a few minutes, they were off the ground quickly gaining altitude enroute to Suwannee County.

Chapter XX

As Warren leveled the small aircraft out around seven thousand feet altitude, he looked over at his reluctant passenger. Warren smiled gently as he noticed Zeb taking in the scenery at such altitude.

"How fast we going?" Zeb yelled over the engine's roar.

"About sixty five miles per hour," Warren answered. "I'll get seventy out of her by myself."

In less than one hour, Warren had spotted some grazing land near Jack's cabin. He circled the prospective makeshift runway a couple of times before making a final approach and landing the aircraft.

After taxiing across the field, Warren finally brought the cub to a complete stop and looked over at Zeb. As Warren McKinley took off his pilot's glasses, Zeb knew some sort of action was about to begin.

"I cannot tell you how important it is to stall Pierce as long as you possibly can, Zeb," Warren instructed.

"How am I going to stall him?" Zeb probed.

"I don't know," Warren said. "That is your job but you don't have an overabundance of time to plan."

"Where you gonna be?" Zeb plainly asked.

"I have to go see someone. Whatever you do, don't let Pierce know I have been here or that you have seen me," warned McKinley.

"Just one thing, Warren," Zeb said before crawling out of the small fuselage.

"Yea, what's that?" Warren replied.

"You didn't have to pull that gun on me," Zeb announced.

"Yes I did," insisted Warren. "Time is of an essence here."

Zeb stared into the distant woods as he reviewed within his mind any questions he may have for Warren McKinley. He realized Warren had a plan and was rapidly learning the younger McKinley brother was in some ways like his brother, Jack. Therefore, he knew Warren would keep him posted on the overall plan, but on a need to know basis.

"Any questions?" Warren asked.

"Just one thing," Zeb replied. "Where do I go after I leave Pierce?"

"If things go as I hope they will," Warren began, "I will get to

Pierce's before you leave. If not, I guess you can plan to attend Jack's funeral and probably mine too."

With that, Warren McKinley revved up the Continental engine in the cub and turned it back in the direction from which he had just taxied. At last, he allowed the plane to start moving and within seconds, he was soaring again. Zeb watched as Warren McKinley turned his craft to the east and flew out of site.

When Zeb could no longer see the airplane, he began his journey by foot to see Scott Pierce. He realized he would have to be very clever in effort of preventing Pierce's suspicions arising.

It was a four mile hike for Zeb to make by road to the home of Scott Pierce. He could easily make that in ninety minutes he realized. By doing so, it would be only two o'clock in the afternoon when he arrived there. That would be far more than two hours of stalling Pierce. He was willing to attempt such a task for maybe an hour but wasn't going to try for two plus hours.

At last, Zeb decided to walk to The Club Palmetto and remain there for one hour. Then he would continue on to see Scott Pierce. At least he had a little time to plan his conversation with Pierce.

As for Warren McKinley, he was in flight to Jacksonville. It was there he hoped to see Sam Pierce, father of Scott. Scott Pierce was a fool and Warren knew it. However, Warren knew there was a single person that could control the madman. That single person was Sam Pierce.

True enough, Warren was involved with Sam in an illegal numbers operation. But in actuality Pierce owed Warren McKinley nothing. Warren had however always found the senior Pierce to be a reasonable man and was confident he would listen to reason.

As Warren flew beyond Lake City and was nearing Baker County, he lit a Lucky Strike. Undoubtedly he began having second thoughts of attempting to rescue the brother whom he had not spoken with in years. Warren began reminiscing the years of past. There had been good ones and of course bad ones had followed.

As far as who was right and who was wrong, that was simple. Warren knew Jack was wrong and Jack knew Warren was wrong. In actuality, they were both wrong. Warren should have never gambled away the farm. On the same token, Jack should have forgiven his only brother. Both of the McKinley Brothers had been raised to know right from wrong.

The single thing that disturbed Warren about Jack the most was not Jack's hostility toward him. It was the fact Jack had seemingly refused to rebound from his hard luck. Warren had seen his brother as a fighter and a survivor when they were but lads. My what a turn of events Warren thought as the little Piper continued to fly eastward.

There was a time Jack would have been coming to Warren's rescue. As the little cub continued to soar farther east, Warren's memory drifted farther back into time.

When Warren was seventeen years of age, his father had given him an assignment to complete. James McKinley had instructed Warren to ride along the river north of Dowling Park and drive the cattle with the McKinley brand down river to the McKinley farm so that they could cut some cattle out to sell.

Such a responsibility elated Warren. Always before it was either Jack or James himself that had gone out to drive the cattle in for market. It was the first time he had felt included and as an equal.

Warren's enthusiasm was soon squelched. He had ridden out his very first morning with all the supplies one would need for undertaking such a task. Miss Martha had packed for him a supply of food fit for a traveling king. Behind his Bona Allen saddle was a bedroll to provide comfort for the budding cowboy on his overnight excursion. Naturally, the younger McKinley brother had his Winchester rifle placed in his gun pouch.

He had gotten just north of Charles Springs when he found a few scrub cattle with the McKinley brand. Warren circled his horse around the cattle and verified his family's brand. He then began to call out, "Haay, yiiiiii, come on heya."

The cows began to move along as the young cowboy gently and slowly drove them toward the McKinley place. He was very attentive to what he was doing when a couple of undesirables who had tyrant dreams of their own intruded on Warren's range. They quickly raced their horses between Warren and his cattle causing the cows to scatter. They then chased the cows off and circled their horses back to Warren McKinley.

"What are you trying to do, boy?" The larger of the two asked.

"I was attempting to drive our cattle back to our farm," the enraged Warren answered. "What is your motive?" He then demanded.

"Our motive is to keep you from gettin' our cows boy," the second ruffian answered egotistically.

"Those cattle belong to my family," Warren insisted. "If you would have looked you could have seen the McKinley brand."

"Well they belong to us now," the smaller ruffian sarcastically replied. "And you best leave 'em alone, little McKinley boy."

The infuriated Warren looked down at his rifle and began thinking of setting things straight.

"If you think about it, we'll just have to kill ya," said the larger rustler.

"And I'll have to kill you," Jack McKinley called out.

A subtle smile overtook Warren as he recalled the cattle drive incident. He checked all the little aircraft's gauges and then enjoyed the scenery of the Baker County timberlands.

The incident Warren recalled helped him resolve that his trip to see Sam Pierce was indeed warranted. He still owed Jack a few favors.

Again, Warren's memories began to engage as his mind drifted back on the cattle drive incident.

After having a few choice words of advice from a convincing Jack McKinley, two reformed cattle rustlers rode into other parts of the world.

"What are you doing here Jack?" a frustrated Warren asked. "I reckon you and Father knew I couldn't handle it."

A smiling Jack held up a skillet and replied, "I just thought maybe you needed to have this. Ain't you planning to eat fish tonight?"

"I could've handled those two guys, Jack," Warren insisted.

"I know you could have," Jack replied. "I was just afraid of what you were going to do to them."

Jack knew Warren could not have handled the two wranglers and Warren was aware of the fact Jack knew it.

"So you gonna tell Father about it?" Warren asked.

"I don't think anybody needs to know other than me and you," Jack replied with a comforting smile. "You had better get back to work and I had too."

Jack eased his horse beside Warren's and placed the iron skillet in his younger brother's bed roll. As Jack began to turn his horse, Warren called out.

"Jack," Warren said.

"Yea?" Jack answered.

"Thank you," stated Warren.

"For what?" Jack replied.

"You know," Warren sheepishly said.

Jack eased his horse up beside Warren's again and gently smiled as he rubbed his clean shaven jaw.

"Hey, that's what brothers are for," Jack explained. "If the shoe was on the other foot you would be there for me wouldn't you?"

"You bet," Warren quickly said. "I'll always be there for you. Brothers forever."

"Brothers forever," Jack said with a smile and a wink.

Jack McKinley then rode off on his Palomino horse.

Jacksonville was in sight for Warren as he focused back on his mission. He had to fight back a tear after recalling the cattle drive incident. It was worth it though. He no longer had any doubts about what he was doing.

Sam Pierce owned a hotel near the downtown area of Jacksonville.

It was not an operative hotel but rather used solely for his home and office. The hotel was a perfect set up for Pierce. It set on a whopping sixty acre compound with immaculate landscape. Sable and Date Palms provided a tropical look while amaryllis and marigolds provided much color and flamboyance for the Hotel De Tropic compound during the spring and early summer months. Crotons and ripening satsumas graced the grounds and added color for the fall months.

The brick hotel was equipped with twenty upstairs rooms. Each of them were roomy and well maintained. The walls of beaded wood never suffered for paint. Every wall was lined with ornate chair rail while the upper portion of the wall was covered in elegant wallpaper. The lower portions of the walls were of beaded wood and were also freshly painted.

Downstairs was rather enchanting for anyone granted the opportunity to see it. The chandelier filled ballroom was appropriately decorated with live plants with a tropical hint. Dinner tables were suitably arranged to allow for mingling and dancing. Music was usually provided by an eight piece orchestra.

Parties were not uncommon at the Hotel De Tropic. Often there were so many people at them the good times would inevitably spill over into the lobby. The lobby within itself was a sight to behold. Delicate, baroque woodwork was indicative of skill and talent having met to erect a true structural work of art.

The black and white checked tile floors were plainly elegant. As for the ceiling, copper ceiling squares with detailed engraving was breathtaking. In the center of the lobby was a waterfall. The waterfall was an original inclusion of the hotel's structure.

Pierce's land surrounding the Hotel De Tropic was not deep at all. It was however rather lengthy. He had acquired neighboring properties in order to have a lengthy spread so that he could accompany airplane landings and takeoffs.

Warren McKinley was no stranger to the landing strip and once again, he was dropping altitude so that he could allow his tail dragger cub touch down on the grass strip. Upon taxiing to a stop, Warren exited the aircraft and briskly walked into the hotel.

"I'm here to see Sam Pierce," Warren coldly announced to a studious looking gentleman as he walked in the front door of the hotel.

The gentleman stood behind what was formerly the reservation desk. It had however been transformed into a receiving desk for those bold enough to call on one Sam Pierce. It was made of marble and brass. Foot rails were along the bottom.

The gentleman whom Warren addressed looked as if he might have been purchased with the hotel. He looked quite at home behind the elaborate desk. His dark suit was fitting but not too flashy. His little round spectacles contributed to the look of intelligence and his predominately bald head seemed to be more indicative of bad nerves rather than heredity.

"Mr. Pierce is not accepting guests today," the man nervously replied.

"If you don't want the responsibility of his son's death on your hands I suggest you go get 'em and tell him Warren McKinley's here to see him," Warren demanded.

The man left the lobby area after promising to announce Warren's presence to Pierce.

Shortly thereafter, the desk clerk turned receptionist returned accompanied by a rather large and seemingly older gentleman. He was not a typical goon one might expect to be under Pierce's employ but instead a common Jacksonville area man.

"I'm Max," the larger gentleman announced to Warren. "Perhaps I can handle whatever your problem is."

Warren quickly noticed the unconcealed weapon the man had stashed in his shoulder holster. Furthermore, Max's melancholy eyes told him he would not hesitate to use the revolver.

Max did not blatantly stare at Warren's exposed gun but he did not fail to take note of it either.

"Max, I appreciate your offering just the same," Warren said. "But it is urgent I personally see Mr. Pierce."

"I understand," Max replied with a smile. "I am sure you will understand I cannot allow you to wear your weapon in there."

"I figured that," Warren confirmed as he handed over his sidearm. "It is just imperative I speak with Mr. Pierce quickly."

"Very well," Max slowly muttered through his thick gray mustache. "I'll show you the way, Mr. McKinley."

Warren followed Max to an upstairs balcony overlooking the grounds of the Hotel De Tropic. Sam Pierce sat there in his conservative business suit smoking a Cuban Cigar. To compliment the cigar, he was having an after lunch brandy.

"Hello Warren," Pierce said cordial enough. "I hope there is not a problem."

"There is," Warren quickly responded.

"You disappoint me, Warren McKinley," Pierce openly admitted. "For two years now I have invited you to my estate and you failed to accept my invitations."

"Yes sir," Warren agreed with his head slightly hung.

"But today," Pierce continued holding his right index finger up as he stood and faced Warren. "Today you come to my fair home with a problem."

"It is a problem only you can offer a solution for," Warren explained.

"Brandy?" Pierce offered.

"No, thank you," replied Warren. "Not while I am flying."

"I watched you land," Pierce commented. "You handle the airplane with such finesse."

Pierce then pointed toward the other wicker chair as he sat back down to his brandy. As he lifted his glass, Warren was seated.

"O.K., Warren," Pierce began, "what is the problem you have?"

"My brother and your son," Warren candidly replied.

"How does that involve us?" Pierce then asked as he turned his eyes to look over the grounds.

"I do not want to see my brother hurt and frankly do not think you wish to see your son harmed either," Jack plainly stated.

Pierce's full attention and torso quickly turned to Warren McKinley. Warren was right and he knew it. Pierce loved his son very much and had great hope for his otherwise dismal future. It was the plan of Sam Pierce to put Scott on the McKinley farm after winning it in the poker game.

"What is going on with them?" Sam Pierce genuinely asked of Warren McKinley.

Quickly and precisely, Warren explained the events that had transpired with Scott Pierce and the McKinley family members. As he talked, Sam Pierce listened attentively.

"You make it sound like it is all my son's fault, Warren," Sam finally said.

"With all due respect," Warren began, "I can understand anyone not getting along with my brother but what about my sister's family?"

Silence overtook the two gentlemen for a brief period. They stared at one another as if they were two opposing generals contemplating the wage of war. As they continued to stare, Max stood near the door that led out to the balcony.

"Max," Sam Pierce called out.

"Yes, Mr. Pierce," answered Max.

"Leave us in private a moment please, Max," suggested Sam Pierce.

Max fulfilled his employer's command, closing the French Doors behind him as he fully entered the hotel. Warren McKinley and Sam Pierce remained on the balcony to discuss the fate of their own families.

"My sister is not a trouble maker," Warren began in a soft, trembling tone. "We are most sure her husband has been killed in the war and she is left with three children to raise. I cannot allow any man to harass her and her family even if he is your son."

Pierce did not appear shocked by Warren's statement. He simply looked expressionless at Warren and softly bobbed his head up and down.

"Your sister's husband," Sam Pierce replied, "is he not the one that testified against my son, Scott?"

"He is the very one," Warren proudly replied. "I have explained all that to you already, sir."

Sam Pierce's brandy glass was empty. He maintained eye contact with Warren as he refilled the glass and again began sipping.

"Sure you will not have a drink?" Pierce again offered.

"Thanks, but no," Warren solemnly replied.

Sam Pierce stood and walked to the railing around the balcony. He looked about his immaculate grounds and slowly sipped his brandy. He soon turned around and faced Warren McKinley only to offer surprise to his associate. Warren saw a burdened man with extremely sad eyes instead of the cocky villain he had anticipated confronting.

"I love Scott as any father might love his son, Warren," Pierce stated with a somber look about him. "I have tried to give him everything but have failed to control him. He never could understand that in our business, one must keep a low profile. Flamboyance is permissible but remaining low keyed is essential. Every aspect of survival hinges around how low keyed a man can keep, Warren."

Warren listened attentively to what Sam Pierce had to say. After all, Pierce was not lacking in good sense.

"Are you willing to help me defuse the quarrel with Jack and Scott?" Warren asked outright.

Pierce then gazed back across his compound as he took another sip of warm brandy. He then turned back to Warren McKinley and glared with a devious smile.

"I'll help," he said. "But it'll cost you McKinley. Oh, it will cost you."

"What is your proposition?" Warren asked.

"You will deliver twenty-four little eight ounce containers of nitroglycerin to the Gulf of Mexico for me," Pierce announced.

"Nitro?" Warren gulped.

"Stakes too high?" Pierce asked as a bewildered Warren looked at him.

Pierce maintained eye contact with Warren McKinley as Warren carefully considered his option. The eye contact was Pierce's ploy to convince Warren to give in.

"It will be well worth your time, Warren," Pierce said. "How does the deed sound to the farm you lost in that poker game?"

"It is awful risky," an astonished Warren commented.

"I need it there by noon tomorrow," Pierce advised. "It will be going out on ship to Central America. There are a few rebels down there planning an uprise and I was able to get my hands on what they need. The problem is, I don't have time to ship it around the state."

Warren then poured a glass of brandy and took a big gulp as large beads of sweat began to form on his forehead. He was well aware of the dangers of transporting nitroglycerin, especially in a rush. By doing so however, he could reacquire the acreage of his family's farm that had been lost in a poker game some years prior.

"What's your answer?" Pierce asked.

"If I attempt to transport the nitro and something happens," Warren began.

"Your family will be deeded the place and no harm will ever be done to any of them," Pierce promised. "You know my word is good, Warren."

"I know that," Warren confirmed in a nervous tone. "I guess you have a deal Mr. Pierce. Where do we go from here?"

"Suwannee County," Sam Pierce replied with a smile as he and Warren McKinley shook hands.

Chapter XXI

As Thomas steered his new vessel down river, Amos was jabbering about one of Miss Ruby's famous bird sandwiches.

"Just hold on Amos," Thomas replied with a flash of his trademark grin. "We fixin' to ride up on a mullet dinner right now."

"I sure do wish I could get me a bird sandwich like Miss Ruby makes," Amos replied.

As they made their way around the final bend in the river before the fish camp, Thomas saw Zeb's Ford Coupe in the road's ditch. He had no doubt of it being Zebs for he remembered the bent trunk lid.

Thomas made no comment to Amos about the car. Once they docked the little skiff, Thomas ran inside the office to find Blue Thompson invoicing a load of fish for one of the route men.

"Where's Warren?" Thomas frantically asked.

"He had to go away on business," Blue replied. "May be gone for a while."

"Somebody with 'em?" Thomas probed.

"I didn't notice," replied Blue in a carefree tone. "Something wrong, Thomas?"

"Oh, no," Thomas replied distantly. "Where you headed?" The young man addressed the truck driver.

"I have to go to Jasper and White Springs and Lake City," the driver replied.

"Got room for me?" Thomas asked.

The driver chuckled as he looked at Blue. "Yea I got room," he admitted. "But you reckon it'll be O.K. with your folks if you go?"

"I ain't got time to find out," Thomas demanded. "I just have to get to Suwannee County."

"I'm not going to take you until your ma says it's alright," the driver insisted.

"No problem," Thomas conceded with a smile and exited the office.

"Dog gone kid," the driver said. "He thinks I'm crazy? I ain't a gonna have no Rose McKinley Wheeler on me like ugly on an ape."

Blue chuckled as he continued to write out the invoice on the seafood.

As the two gentlemen completed business as usual, Thomas ran to his bed in the bungalow and grabbed a bed sheet. He then scampered back to the fish truck, opened the back door and crawled in quietly closing it behind him. The truck was dark and rather smelly but that didn't matter. It was a quick trip home. Thomas spread the sheet out and lay down placing his jacket over him. He would just have to pay attention to the curves and bumps along the way to gauge where he was.

Within moments, Thomas was experiencing an uncomfortable ride and Amos was in search of his sidekick. Amos looked about the fish camp and around the boat. Needless to say he was getting extremely worried. Thomas was an avid swimmer but Amos still could only think of the worst.

At last, Amos checked inside the office where Blue was sitting with his feet propped up smoking a cigar.

"You seen Thomas?" Amos asked.

"Why is it everybody is looking like crazy for everybody else?" Blue replied. "He was just in here trying to get the Lake City and Jasper route man to give 'em a ride."

"Where's Mister Warren?" Amos probed further.

"He left in a hurry on business," Thompson replied.

Amos and Blue's minds clicked at the same time. They looked at one another as if in disbelief. Amos should have known to believe anything when Thomas Wheeler was involved. Blue on the other hand naturally had no reason to be so suspecting of the lad.

"Why did the kid get in such an all fired hurry to go back to Suwannee County today?" Blue asked as he and Amos walked outside.

Amos looked about one hundred yards down the road and pointed toward Zeb's Ford Coupe.

"That's why," he replied. "Looks like the trouble at home done boiled up to a head. I gotta get there."

"Oh, no," Blue argued. "You are going to have to tell Rose that her son is on the fish truck 'cause I ain't tellin' her. She can be plum mean."

"Miss Rose be a good lady," Amos stated as he turned and walked away. "But I sure 'nuff hate to be the one that has to tell her 'bout that mean boy she got," he added under his breath so that Blue could not hear.

Amos had a score of his own to settle with Pierce. Every time he laughed, coughed, woke up, rolled over in bed, or just breathed he was reminded of the broken ribs. He wanted revenge and he wanted it badly. Amos was however knowledgeable of how important it was for him to remain with the McKinley's at the Bay.

Meanwhile Jack McKinley remained alone at the Wheeler Place awaiting his adversaries arrival. Everything was somewhat in order he assumed. Jack was by no means scared but was perhaps becoming a little anxious to get the whole mess over with. Thomas Wheeler had somehow influenced him to live again and he was ready to do so.

Jack poured out all the gas he could find so that nobody could have fuel on hand to torch the place. Outside, he had strategically placed small mirrors around the buildings so that he could have added vision in case Pierce's goons decided to do a little sneaking around.

Four o'clock in the afternoon was rapidly approaching so he decided to take a final stroll around the small outbuildings behind the house. As he walked into the barn, he heard something suspicious. The barn was open in the center. On one side were three stalls where animals were often kept. The noise seemed to have came from one of the outside stalls.

Jack slowly pulled a fillet knife from his vest and quietly walked to the stall. He did not want to risk alarming his foes with the loud blast of his revolver. Jack stooped down toward the dirt floor and peered through the slats to see a man's feet. It was obvious the man in the stall too was slumped down so that he may not be seen.

The partition that separated the open area from the stall was only four feet high. Jack considered the man was most likely armed but he also realized he could be on top of his enemy before he knew it. Therefore, a careless Jack McKinley was airborne and soared over the wall. Indeed he did land atop the other man.

Jack's adversary was unarmed and quite unnerved as he focused with his single eye on the long filleting blade at the tip of his nose. The man was terribly frightened but was by no means an intruder.

In near shock, Jack looked at the mangled Charles Wheeler.

"Charles Wheeler?" Jack asked. "When did you come back?"

"I am not back," Charles snapped. "I will be leaving."

"Where are you going?" Jack asked in growing concern.

"It doesn't matter," a frustrated Charles replied. "I'm just going. I can not stay like this."

"Oh, no," Jack said as he attempted to keep focused on his own approaching embattlement.

"You going to tell Rose?" Charles asked.

"Look," Jack said, "there is a lot going on right now, Charles, that I don't think you know about. We need to get inside quick."

Jack escorted his brother-in-law inside. The two men sat down at the kitchen table and Jack poured them each a cup of coffee. They then shared the events with each other that had taken place over the past few years and what had led them to where they presently were.

Charles reluctantly explained to Jack how he had been injured while handling explosives in Italy. The accident had claimed Charles Wheeler's left arm and eye. It also affected his left leg. The doctors had done very well in saving the mangled leg Charles explained to Jack. He further added he had been in a military hospital for several months and was released.

Jack on the other hand explained to Charles the troubles with Scott Pierce.

"I knew something was up when I realized you were staying here. I then drifted down to the bay and saw my family down there," Charles admitted. "Thomas has made a man. You know, he just about saw me."

"So you were just going to leave my sister and the three beautiful children ya'll have?" An angered Jack asked.

"I have a better excuse than you had," Charles retaliated with a trembling voice. "Look at me Jack!"

"It doesn't matter," Jack said. "So you were injured. You just going to give up?"

"Well ain't that just the pot calling the kettle black," Charles angrily stated. "Jack didn't you give up on everything after losing the baby and Stella getting sick and then Warren gambled away the farm?"

"Leave Stella out of it," Jack retaliated.

"That's right," Charles sadistically said, "you've left her out of everything. As far as you're concerned, she died when the baby died."

Jack then rose to his feet with his fists clinched. He fiercely gritted his teeth as his morbid eyes of fire glazed at Charles Wheeler.

"Why I outta.....," he began.

"Go ahead," Charles readily replied as he stood up with the help of a walking stick. "Will it make you feel good to hit me Jack? Still the same old Jack I see. Using your fists instead of your heart."

Jack set down and held his head. Charles couldn't be certain but was favorably sure his rugged brother-in-law was actually weeping. It was definitely a moment of reckoning for two Suwannee County men.

"Things haven't been easy have they, Charles?" A somber Jack asked rhetorically.

"No," Charles replied with a gentle smile.

Jack then realized where young Thomas had gotten his contagious smile from. It was Charles that had given him that quality.

Jack then smiled at Charles and said, "I have a deal for you, Charles Wheeler. You face your family the way you are and I will face Stella."

Before Charles could answer, Jack quickly raced to the window. He saw Scott Pierce's car coming up the drive.

"Go to the bedroom!" Jack commanded Charles.

"I will be the one facing Pierce," Charles said authoritatively.

Jack McKinley quickly glanced about the kitchen. He then ran into one of the bedrooms and returned hastily with a bed sheet. Jack then removed his pearl handled pocket knife and cut a small strip of approximately three feet in length. He then cut another the same size. Finally, Jack cut a third strip. The third strip was longer.

"Come here then. I need your help," Jack said to Charles as he began walking back to the bedroom.

Charles followed behind him. When they got into the room, Jack caught Charles looking at Rose's portrait and quickly punched him in the forehead. Instantly, Wheeler fell to the bed and Jack used the cutting from the bed sheet to gag him and tie him up.

"I'm so sorry, Charles," a regretful Jack said as he looked at his knocked out brother-in-law.

By the time Jack got back into the living room, there was a knock on the door. He then rushed to the kitchen and pulled down a bottle of whiskey. Jack gargled the liquor and placed the bottle on the table. He then laid his head down on the dining table.

After he heard another knock, the door opened and he estimated four men enter the house.

"Jack McKinley. You in here?" Zeb called out.

Zeb's presence threw Jack off guard. He was not anticipating Zeb to be with Pierce. Jack had to wonder if his friend might be double crossing him. Nonetheless, Jack played the part of a drunk as the men waltzed on into the offset kitchen where he sat.

"Well hello, Mr. McKinley," Scott Pierce said in a sarcastic tone.

"What do you want and who invited you in?" Jack replied with matching sarcasm.

McKinley and his two associates seated themselves backward in the remaining three straight chairs around the wooden dinette table where Jack sat. Pierce occupied the chair directly across from McKinley.

"I want to beat you to a pulp and then kill you. That is what I want," Pierce said. "But instead, I am going to buy your interest in The Club Palmetto."

"And if I don't want to sell?" Jack asked innocently.

"Zeb," snapped Pierce.

Zeb then pulled a snub nose revolver from his inner coat pocket and held it to McKinley's head. Zeb then began laughing as he pressed the short barrel down into Jack's ear.

"I likes this," Zeb said through gritted teeth. "Oh yea you real tough with a pistol poked in your ear ain't you Jack McKinley."

"I think your old buddy Zeb here wants to kill you," Pierce said with his cynical grin.

"So it seems," a confused Jack replied.

The five men sat in silence for moments. Little did four of them know Charles Wheeler was in the bedroom. Jack was concentrating on just how he was going to get out of the mess he was in. He felt sure he could shoot all of them and maybe get shot only once or twice. It was that one or two times he worried about though. That's all the bullets it would take. Furthermore, he knew Zeb's capabilities with a gun. Zeb was by no means a slouch.

The main problem facing Jack was Zeb. If Zeb was on his side he sure didn't want to shoot him. However, if he had double crossed Jack then Zeb would need to be the first shot because of his shooting expertise. Jack knew he was good for he had taught him.

Chapter XXII

While Jack McKinley was being held at gun point by Scott Pierce and company, Warren and Sam Pierce were rapidly approaching southern Suwannee County. Also, Thomas Wheeler was nearing the place with James McKinley and Amos not far behind him. When they realized where he had gone, they too followed.

As James drove, Amos couldn't help but wonder what he had meant at the bay when he said it was time he settled things he should have settled thirty-five years ago.

James McKinley was perhaps the most humble man that people from Suwannee County or Dead Man's Bay had ever encountered. Naturally when he said something the least unordinary, people heeded the contents of his words. James McKinley was also known to honor his and his family's word, whatever the sacrifice may be.

When the fish truck stopped in Luraville at the cold storage, Thomas was able to slip out undetected and began walking to the Wheeler place approximately four miles up river. Much to his surprise, James and Amos soon came along and picked him up. The timing could not have been more precise for when they were pulling up the lane to the Wheeler home, Warren McKinley was landing his small aircraft in the pasture his family had one time owned.

"Land it in the pasture," Sam Pierce said. "It'll soon be yours again."

"If we're not too late," a concerned Warren added.

Inside the house the sound of the plane added just enough diversion for Jack McKinley to make his move. He had no idea the plane was going to land or who was even in it for that matter so he did what he knew to do.

As Scott Pierce and his two sidekicks glared out the window, to catch a glimpse of the aircraft, Jack caught a reassuring smile come over Zeb's face. Jack nodded and Zeb quickly knocked the goon that was next to him in the back of the head with his revolver. As Pierce and the other goon quickly turned, Zeb poked the gun in the stomach of the goon. Jack had already easily drawn his own revolver and was pointing it at Scott Pierce.

"Now look who's in charge," Jack said without expression. "All of you on the floor."

Of course one of them was already on the floor rubbing his aching head as Scott Pierce remained standing with a belligerent look overcoming him.

"Now!" Jack exclaimed as the men all laid flat on the floor and Zeb pat searched them and took their weapons.

"You double crossed me, nigger," Scott said as Zeb searched him.

"I sho 'nuff did," Zeb replied with a smile. "I'm just surprised as all get out you thought I would double cross Mr. Jack. "You one fool white man."

"Keep 'em at bay," Jack instructed Zeb. "We have more company out there."

"It's Mr. Warren," Zeb proudly said.

It was a look of anger Zeb had never seen on Jack. Jack quickly ran about the room positioning the windows for gunfight as he loaded his vest pockets with the weapons of those adversaries on the floor.

"I should have known he was part of this," Jack muttered in repulsion.

"He's here for you, Mr. Jack," Zeb softly said. "I went after him."

"What gave you that right?" Jack demanded.

"This is the time to heal, Jack!" Zeb said in a tone of voice he had never used with Jack McKinley. "You have to let the past go and start anew."

"I would have rather died," McKinley replied as he walked out the back door to the barn and left Zeb holding Pierce and company at gunpoint.

Jack had no intention of turning back. His full intent was to keep walking. At that point he wanted out of Suwannee County, North Florida, and the McKinley family. What caught his attention was the forty two panel wagon of his father's pulling up the lane.

James McKinley got out of the wagon and began walking to meet Warren and Sam Pierce McKinley as they were getting off the airplane. Jack paused and watched for only a brief moment but decided now was the time to leave. His work was done.

"Uncle Jack! Uncle Jack!" Thomas shouted. "Wait on me Uncle Jack!"

Jack stopped and watched his nephew run toward him. When Thomas reached him, he jumped up and bear hugged Jack McKinley.

"I was so worried about you, Uncle Jack. I was coming to help you," Thomas said as Zeb escorted Scott Pierce and company outside.

Jack was at a loss for words. He placed his left hand on his knee and bent down wiping Thomas' large tears away with his right hand.

"I want you to go inside through the back door," Jack said. "I have a package in there for you. Look inside your ma's bedroom. I have it tied up like a gift on the floor. Now it's old and beat up but it's all yours. Run along now."

Thomas looked a bit confused but agreed to do so. As he walked toward the house, Jack smiled as he fought back a few tears of his own.

"Thomas," Jack called out.

"Yes sir?" the lad replied.

"Promise me you'll always take care of it?" Jack asked.

"I promise," Thomas replied not knowing just how great the gift was.

Jack continued his intended journey. To his north was Warren and Sam walking from the airplane. To his south was James McKinley walking briskly to meet them. Beside James McKinley's car stood Amos.

No matter how bad Jack wanted to continue his walk, he couldn't. It had been several months since he had seen his father. He simply could not shun his own father at that point. Once again, Jack McKinley paused his walk and awaited the approach of his father.

"Hello, Pa," Jack said.

"Son," James replied in a distant but yet warm manner.

"I'm leaving now, Pa," Jack said.

"No, wait son," James instructed.

Like a good son, Jack remained as his father had instructed. Over the years, Jack McKinley had often avoided his father. It was not out of dislike but rather respect. Jack's way of living was somewhat more relaxed in a sense than James McKinley's. Therefore, the younger McKinley had simply preferred not to disappoint his father. Heaven knows James never approved of the drinking, gambling, fighting, and general carousing about North Florida that Jack had succumbed to. Nor had James and Martha approved of Warrens shortcomings either.

"Yes, Pa," Jack softly answered awaiting further instruction.

"I think you should be present for the conversation about to take place son," James advised. "And then you are free to go where you please and as you please."

Within only a few seconds, Warren McKinley and Sam Pierce were present. Sam and James stood and faced one another eye to eye. Standing back a short distance centered between them and off to each side was Jack and Warren McKinley. Naturally they stood on opposite sides of James and Sam.

For a lengthy moment, Sam and James stared at one another. It seemed to be stares of regret. As they stared at one another, Warren and Jack would occasionally catch a glimpse of each other as well.

When Warren looked into Jack's eyes, he detected Jack had lost something over time. Perhaps it was that self confidence that had always gleamed through Jack's eyes of blue. Nonetheless there had always been a positive glow about Jack that Warren found time to have erased.

"What will it take for all of this to stop, Sam?" James asked.

"I would like for it to stop now," Sam admitted. "You know I always resented you, James. I was jealous of the relationship you and Father had."

"Jealous of me?" James asked. "But it was you he always seemed to care for most."

"Oh, no," Sam insisted. "It was me he had to help most. I was the troubled one. I ran with the wrong crowd and did the wrong things. All I could ever hear him say was you should be more like my younger boy, James. I just wanted to hurt you," a tearful Sam Pierce McKinley admitted.

"I am truly sorry, Sam," James said as his two astonished sons looked on.

By then Warren and Jack had figured out that James McKinley and Sam Pierce shared the same father. Never before did they realize it though.

"No, James," Sam said "you have nothing to be sorry for. I am the one that has tried to ruin your family. They have pulled together and proved to me that you have raised them not to be destroyed."

"I think we still need to work on the two boys," James added as his eyes cut at Jack and then Warren.

Jack and Warren then looked at one another. Warren was willing to resolve their differences. Jack on the other hand would not be so willing. Warren could easily tell just by the way Jack looked at him.

"Warren," Sam began. "I stalked you like a panther might stalk a pig. I knew you were James's boy and used you to hurt him. That is why I wanted you involved in my numbers business. Finally I figured I could really induce pain by winning your pa's farm in a poker game. Anyhow, I'm truly sorry for what I have done."

Warren then hung his head for there was still no glory in the situation for him. Meanwhile, a bitter Jack continued to glare with malice at his only brother.

Sam Pierce McKinley then extended his hand to James McKinley. The men then shook hands and at last fully accepted one another as brothers.

"I suppose you two would like to know how Sam is your uncle," James commented. "Well here's how it was. Our father was a railroad man. He was up in New York City when he fell in love with a beautiful Italian lady. The problem was Papa was an Irishman. As you boys may or may not know, the Italian and Irish settlers have always clashed so her family would not permit her to marry an Irishman."

The boys listened attentively as Sam also listened to the sad story of his own origin.

"They ran Papa out of New York," James continued. "The railroad relocated him down here in Florida. Well you all know what happened next. He tried to forget about Sam's mother, Sophia and married my mother. Little did Papa know he not only left Sophia, but he had left an unborn baby as well. A few years later, Papa found out through a fellow railroad worker."

"How did he get the name Pierce?" Warren asked.

"My mother married a drunkard named Pierce. Her father arranged the marriage to give me a name," Sam sadly stated. "The arrangement was a disaster. Meanwhile our father was flourishing here in Florida and I felt deprived from all of that."

"Why didn't you tell us about this, Pa?" Warren pleaded to his father.

"I have felt the pain of having a brother that I could not talk to nearly all my life," James explained. "I didn't want my family having to deal with the pain too. I guess I felt by avoiding the problem it would go away. I was wrong boys. If you have a problem you should deal with it."

Meanwhile, Thomas had walked into his mother's bedroom where he discovered his precious father on the floor all tied up. Thomas gulped as a variety of emotions swarmed his soul when he saw Charles.

"Pa," Thomas called out timidly. "Pa, is it you?"

Charles's sad eye focused on his oldest son as Thomas knelt down and carefully untied his father with tender love.

"Papa," Thomas said as he removed the gag Jack had placed over his mouth, "they have hurt you."

Thomas embraced his father as Charles wept profusely.

"It is O.K.," Charles insisted. "They can not hurt me any more."

"Are you home now for good?" The young man candidly asked his wounded father.

"That all depends," Charles answered earnestly.

"On what?" replied an eager Thomas.

"Can you all handle me being like this?" Charles asked.

"Pa," Thomas said with large trickling tears. "that doesn't matter. We just want you home with us."

"Let's go get your ma and Nancy and Allen," Charles said.

Sam and James McKinley had begun walking toward the house. Warren followed behind them as Jack remained gazing about the fields he had once worked diligently.

"What now?" James asked his brother, Sam Pierce.

"Well," Sam replied with a humble smile. "I am going to see if they will let me take my boy back to Jacksonville. I have my work cut out for me, James. May I speak with you in private concerning that land?" Sam added as he pointed toward the acreage he had acquired in the poker game.

"You may," James replied as the two sauntered toward the house.

Much to the surprise of Warren and James, Thomas exited the house with Charles Wheeler. It was an enchanting moment.

"Look, Grandpa, it's Pa!" Thomas yelled with tears of joy steadily streaming. "He's home!"

Jack McKinley savored the moment. He observed the husband and son of his sister as they experienced a reunion so joyous words could never describe. He then watched the courageous Zeb as he continued to hold the villains at gun point. Next, Jack turned his attention to his father and Sam Pierce. It was comforting for him to know an old hatchet was going to be buried after too many years of anguish. Finally Jack looked at Warren. After glaring at his brother for a few seconds, he turned and waved at Amos.

Jack McKinley then walked away from it all.

Chapter XXIII

It had certainly been a tense afternoon at the Wheeler home. Somehow all the anticipated adversity and torment did not have to be. There was no gunfire nor was there bloodshed. Some differences had been resolved and promises of peace had been made.

Zeb released Scott Pierce and his two associates at the request of Sam and James. From there they would quickly pack, under Sam's direction and they would accompany Sam to Jacksonville. Sam intended to spend much time at the Hotel De Tropic devoting most of that time to Scott.

James, Amos, Charles, and Thomas would all travel to Dead Man's Bay where a joyous reunion was inevitable. Warren still had much work to do for he had made a deal with Sam Pierce.

Sam and James did talk in private. After their brief meeting, James walked outside where Warren stood beneath a pecan tree hulling and eating a few pecans that Thomas would not get.

"Warren," James said. "I understand you have made a deal with Sam."

"I have, Father," Warren replied.

James McKinley nodded his head with a somber look overcoming him. He then picked up a couple of pecans and crushed them together in his hand. He hulled one of the pecans out and placed it in his mouth.

"Kind of dangerous isn't it?" James asked.

"Reckon so," Warren replied. "I'll be O.K."

"Look over there at Charles," James said to Warren. "That is what explosives can do, son."

"Father," Warren said respectfully, "please do not make this any more difficult for me than it already is. My stomach is already tied in knots just thinking of what can happen should I experience excessive turbulence."

"You do not have to do this," James replied.

"I do," Warren stated, "and you know why."

Warren then had a moment in private with Sam to receive instructions of flying the cargo to the Gulf.

"Where do I pick up the nitro?" Warren asked.

Sam gave Warren explicit instructions of what to do once he reached Jacksonville. He then confirmed there would be a boat awaiting him at Dead Man's Bay.

"You do know Donavon Brantley?" Sam asked.

"I do," Warren replied.

Ironically Donavon had roots in Suwannee County and spent most of his time ashore in Steinhachee. He was a quite a character as well. Donavon looked as rough as any pirate Warren had ever known but was however highly regarded among those who knew him. Primarily a rum runner, Brantley would transport just about anything on his ship as would many of the large boat owners along the gulf coast.

"Good," said Sam. "He will take the stuff off your hands and deliver it to South America."

Sam told Warren there was to be a revolution take place in a small South American country. They had contacted him about the nitroglycerin and he was selling.

"I think it is a good cause," Sam added. "Everyone will be expecting you. Anyway if you have any questions, I will see you at my Hotel in Jacksonville later tonight."

Warren McKinley and Sam Pierce shook on the deal and went their separate ways. Sam accompanied his son and their employees to take their possessions from the farm house so that it may be turned back over to the McKinley's.

Warren spent a few minutes with Charles before preparing to fly to Jacksonville.

"That's some boy you have there, Charles," Warren said.

"Oh, I know," Charles replied. "We have a lot of catching up to do."

Warren then sought advise from Charles in transporting the nitroglycerin. He figured Charles could at least tell him what not to do.

"If it jars it will explode," Charles warned. "You have to handle the stuff like a newborn baby. I wouldn't do it if I were you, Warren. But if you are going to, I will help."

"Thanks, but no," Warren replied appreciatively. "I must do it alone."

"It's awful risky," Charles said shaking his head.

"Warren forced a smile and simply replied, "I know, Charles, I know."

Warren McKinley then turned to walk toward his aircraft but paused.

"Charles," he called out.

"Yes, Warren," Charles replied.

"Only you and Father know of what I am doing. I would like to keep it that way if you don't mind," Warren said.

"Very well," Charles agreed. "Be careful."

The Pierces were first to leave the Wheeler place. As they got to the end of the lane, Sam looked down the road a way and saw Jack afoot headed in the direction of The Club Palmetto.

Sam instructed Scott, who was driving to carry him to Jack. As the car pulled up beside Jack McKinley, Jack reached inside his vest as he was forced to maintain a certain amount of skepticism of Pierce.

Sam got out of the car and held his hands up, palm out stating, "I am not trying anything funny, Jack."

"What do you want?" Jack asked.

"I want you to enjoy having your place back," Sam said.

"I don't follow," Jack replied.

"It's all been worked out," Sam Pierce explained. "Your brother is flying some nitroglycerin for me to Dead Man's Bay. In return, I am deeding the place back to your father."

Jack was stunned. He knew Warren had no knowledge of flying explosives. Furthermore such an attempt was nothing short of suicidal.

"I thought you were going to leave us alone," Jack said.

"Warren and I had already made the deal," Sam said. "Oh he'll be fine. Besides you don't like him that much anyway."

Jack just stared as Sam Pierce smiled at him. It was an unsettling feeling for Jack. There was however nothing he could do for Warren had made his own choices in life and was clearly his own man.

"Well, either way it's on Warren," Jack said as Sam got back into the car.

As the sedan began driving away, it stopped and Sam rolled down his window.

"Oh, just one more thing, Jack," he said. "Did you ever hear about the night of the poker game that Warren lost the farm?"

"Never cared to," Jack replied bitterly.

"He was attempting to acquire a home I owned in Chattahoochee," Sam said. "It was important to him. He said he wanted to acquire it for you so that you could be close to you wife."

Jack never answered. The car drove away as he stood there in sorrow. Jack never knew it was for him Warren had gambled the farm away.

He then heard the bellow of the small Piper Cub and watched it ascend into the Eastern skies.

"Warren!" Jack screamed out to no avail. "Don't, Warren, please don't!"

Jack McKinley then burst into tears and wept uncontrollably as he fell to the sandy road. Remorse overwhelmed him for he had breached all relations for over ten years with the brother that loved him so.

Chapter XXIV

As the Piper Cub soared out of sight, Jack recalled his brother's infatuation with airplanes even as a mere child. Warren always dreamed of piloting aircraft through the skies.

"One day, I will fly all the way from the Atlantic to the Gulf," Warren once told Jack.

Jack could only hope he would make his cross state flight back to the bay. Nothing had ever seemed easy for Warren. He always wanted to do good for others but had always seemed to come up short. No doubt he was a good business man but had somehow been jinxed in the business of good deeds.

The weather however did appear to be in Warren's favor that particular day. The humidity was low and the air was not so heavy which offered a smoother ride for the cub. As far as rain, it did not look likely at all. In fact, Warren rather enjoyed the clear skies. It was flying at it's best. He was a little nervous about the fact he had to transport the nitroglycerin back to the bay but had conceded to the fact whatever would be would be.

Sam Pierce had given Warren specific instructions to see Max at Hotel De Tropic in Jacksonville. Max would be expecting Warren and would have the cargo loaded on the small aircraft for flight.

Warren had until noon the following day to deliver the goods and the weather conditions was ideal for such a perilous adventure. Dark however would soon be closing in on him. He decided to lay over in Jacksonville for the night and take off at the break of dawn the next day with his cargo of explosives.

After just over an hour in flight, Warren had the airstrip at the Hotel De Tropic in sight. There, he made his final landing of the day and fueled the small plane up so that he could fly out early the next morning.

As for the ladies of Dead Man's Bay, they were all rather testy. Blue Thompson had shared his little knowledge with them of the men folks' whereabouts.

"Why I am going to lay down the law to little Mr. Thomas Wheeler when I see him again," Rose announced.

"Why on earth would he just run off like that?" Martha asked genuinely as they rocked in the wicker rockers upon the front porch of the large bungalow.

"I know why," Melanie chimed in with a smile. "Because Thomas is a nephew to Sir Warren McKinley."

Martha smiled lovingly at her daughter-in-law as the three ladies continued to rock as if tomorrow would not be. Each of the ladies was concerned of what might be taking place but all refused to admit that concern. They were indeed three strong ladies mustering additional strength for one another.

Allen and Nancy played peacefully around the crab traps between the bungalow and the fish camp. They were still young enough to ignore the troubles anyone else could easily be plagued with. Rose realized one of the beauties of youth is the absence of awareness of those problems impending.

"They are going to be a little more respectful of my feelings," Rose said confidently as she pointed at the little ones at play.

"Thomas cares more than I think you realize, Rose," her mother said softly. "All he is trying to do is keep things going while his father is gone."

"Yes, and that is not all the little worm is up to," Rose revolted. "He is bent and determined to have my brothers act like brothers again."

A glow of happiness suddenly burst out in Melanie's eyes. She smiled slightly but appeared as if she was holding back laughter of joy.

"I was afraid Thomas didn't like Warren," Melanie said.

"Oh, honey," Rose replied. "Thomas very much likes Warren."

"He hasn't always cared that much for him though," Melanie commented in a melancholy tone.

Martha did not comment. Rose however grabbed Melanie's hand and gently squeezed it.

"I think Thomas finally got to know Warren when they went to Jug Island," Rose explained. "The boat did not buy Thomas' friendship. I think it was more so the rattlesnake."

"Rattlesnake?" Martha gulped.

"I didn't hear anything about the rattlesnake," Melanie commented.

"They didn't tell me either," Rose said. "I happened up on Thomas talking to Allen and Nancy."

A peaceful smile then overtook the weary face of Rose McKinley Wheeler as she thought of her three children.

"Thomas was telling the children about the snake?" Martha probed.

"Yes," Rose continued. "You see, ever since Charles has been gone, Thomas talks with the other two children each night. He tells them the important events of the day and what his plans are the following day. He didn't know I heard him the other night when he was telling about the rattlesnake that Warren stumbled upon in the woods when they went to Jug Island."

"Heavens alive," Martha said as her body shivered. "I am scared to death of them things."

"Well," Rose went on, "Thomas killed the snake. He told Allen and Nancy about it and was explaining to them how important it is to do what Uncle Warren says. Oh, he told them what a good man Warren McKinley is and how much he has on his mind."

Melanie smiled gently as she only wanted her husband accepted by others for the good man he really was.

"He told them how lucky they all were to have Warren and Jack McKinley for uncles," Rose finally added.

"And Thomas talks to them every night?" Martha asked with pride.

"Every night," Rose answered. "He don't know I know but you know what he's been doing Mama?"

"There's not a bit of telling," Martha replied.

"He's been breaking horses for the Captain," Rose blurted. "Of course I'm not supposed to know about it. Can you believe that?"

"Oh, yes I can," said Martha. "Why that sounds just like his other uncle, Jack."

Melanie joined Rose in laughter as they continued to await the return of the men folk. The ladies were all aware of the trouble brewing with Scott Pierce but was unaware that particular problem had been solved. What they were unaware of though was Warren's pending flight with explosives.

Chapter XXV

An eerie quiet was accompanying the fall of night at Dead Man's Bay. Silence among the ladies had become prominent. The only dominant sound during those tense moments was that of ham frying in the iron skillet. Melanie had decided to prepare supper for everyone as she was in much hopes everyone would come home.

All Melanie knew about Warren's whereabouts was what Blue had told her. She did however believe he was with his father and brother. Time would however have to pass before she could know, Melanie realized.

Melanie was also cooking grits and eggs. The responsibility of cornbread had been given to Rose. While Rose and Melanie prepared supper, Martha occupied the front porch with her two youngest grandchildren.

At last, Martha heard the familiar sound of the panel wagon James had driven off that day. She hurriedly sent the little ones inside and anxiously stood beside the wood column that suspended the roof over the front porch. Martha was becoming increasingly tense as she wrung her hands awaiting word of what might have transpired.

The wagon rolled to a stop and Thomas exited the driver's door.

"Get Ma," Thomas called to his grandmother with his smile.

"Thomas are all of you O.K.?" Martha demanded.

"Aw, Grandma, we just couldn't be better," the young man answered as Amos and James got out of the car.

Martha, still a little nervous, went inside to get Rose. As she was inside requesting Rose's presence outside, Charles Wheeler stepped outside of the wagon and Thomas stood beside him. There they awaited Rose's exit.

In only a moment's time, Rose walked out on the front porch wiping her hands with a dish rag. The faded dress of pastel print she wore had remained in Charles's memory throughout his years away.

Rose stood still for a moment as she and Charles looked at one another. Thomas was smiling as were James and Amos. Somehow Charles and Rose were caught up in a trance of disbelief as they both savored that particular moment each of them had long awaited.

Martha slipped up behind Rose and said, "Go to your husband, Rose. I think he needs you."

No words were said for a while. Charles and Rose stood embraced as Thomas went inside to escort his younger brother and sister to their father.

"Come on," Thomas said to Allen and Nancy who happened to be drawing pictures of boats in the dining room. "Our papa wants to see ya'll."

"Papa's here?" Nancy gulped with wide opened eyes.

"He sure is," Thomas replied. "Ya'll come on and see 'em."

The moment of joy went on for some time as a family was again complete. Eventually Charles would tell Rose of his skepticism about returning due to his injuries.

Naturally Rose would simply, truthfully and tearfully reply to his skepticism, "We love you as you are."

Melanie also shared in the joy of Charles's return but looked on the cheerful reunion with a feeling of emptiness. She was very concerned about Warren but did not want to take the others' joy away by demonstrating her deep concern.

At last James McKinley spoke. "I would like to talk with everyone in the living room for just a moment," he said in a tone that was over-shadowed with concern.

"It's Warren isn't it?" Melanie replied as she was no longer able to conceal her raging fears within.

"He's alright," James promised, "but please, allow me to explain what is going on with him."

Everyone went inside and found a place to set. Upon Martha carrying coffee to James, he made eye contact with each individual in the room. At last he began talking.

"Sam Pierce and I are brothers," he began candidly. "That is why he has been in our lives to the degree he has. Now I knew all along we were brothers but just never felt like talking about it. There had always been bad blood between us."

James McKinley did not try to coat his speech with sugar. He was very direct and honest. Nor did he demonstrate emotions of any extreme.

"So where is Warren," Melanie anxiously asked.

"Warren is probably at Sam's place in Jacksonville," James said as he sympathetically looked at Melanie.

Chill bumps appeared on Melanie's arms as James paused and

looked at Martha. He attempted to give them each a smile of comfort and encouragement but was unsuccessful in doing so.

"Why is he there, James?" Martha demanded.

"Warren is going to fly some nitroglycerin to the gulf for Sam," James openly told. "In return, the place goes back to our family."

"There is no place worth the life of my son," said Martha in a cutting tone. "I cannot believe you allowed this to happen."

"He is to be home tomorrow morning," James replied. "I am quite sure everybody wanted to know where Warren is. Well, now you know."

As Rose stared at her father in dissatisfaction Charles spoke up. "Mr. McKinley tried to discourage Warren from doing this."

"It's O.K. Charles," James said as he meandered to the door. "I know how they feel. I'm feeling the same pain they are right now. Oh, and if anybody wants to know where Jack is, your guess is as good as mine."

James McKinley walked out to the river and prayed that one day his family might understand everything. He sat there for moments reminiscing on the days he and his sons caught speckled trout from that very river.

Jack was the better fisherman and did it with such finesse, James quietly recalled. Ironically Jack didn't care all that much about fishing but Warren on the other hand dearly loved it. Jack realized that and would intentionally let many fish get away just so his younger brother could reap the joys of catching the most. James had no idea if that brotherly love would ever return.

"Grandpa," Thomas said, "you O.K.?"

"Hey, Thomas," James replied without looking up. "I'm alright."

"Grandpa, I ain't mad with ya," the young man thoughtfully said. "Besides Uncle Warren is probably the best pilot there is. He'll be O.K."

"I know it," James said.

"Well Grandpa, I'm going back in there where my pa is," Thomas said as he left James McKinley alone on the river's bank. James' thoughts returned to the family farm and wondered if he made the right decision to sign the deed when Warren told him of his fate of the poker game. Yes the sacrifice was worth the honor of his son's word. "Yes, I made the right decision," James silently conceded.

The McKinley bungalow was filled that particular evening with a host of mixed emotions. Some emotions in the air were happy and some sad while others were angry and frightful.

"How were you injured Charles?" Rose finally asked.

"I was handling nitroglycerin and it expl..." Charles began but did not finish.

"Go ahead and say it," Melanie said as her voice began to quiver. "It exploded."

"That's about the size of it," Charles confirmed as Melanie stormed out of the bungalow in tears.

"I shouldn't have said that I reckon," Charles told Rose.

Rose didn't reply. She only went over to Charles and gently kissed him. He held her with his single arm as her tears trickled down to his shoulder.

Martha fed Allen and Nancy but as for everyone else, their appetites had been suppressed. Thomas quietly remained in the kitchen nibbling cornbread and sipping coffee. Martha went to her room and the kids soon went to bed. Charles and Rose were inseparable as they talked non stop in the living room. As for James McKinley, he experienced loneliness as he never had on the river bank until the wee hours of morning.

Warren had fueled his plane and was sipping coffee from the balcony of the Hotel De Tropic. He had already spoken with Sam Pierce and received all instructions for the morning's task. Warren had also enjoyed a meal consisting of steamed shrimp, baked fish, baked sweet potatoes, grits. Palm salad served as appetizer and dessert.

The air was not too uncomfortably cool to enjoy out that evening but Warren decided to go back in and write Melanie a letter just in case. She had been very understanding having been continuously subjected to his spur of the moment trips and meetings over the years. Rarely had she been given notice of any changes that might have occurred in their schedules. Melanie had never complained but Warren knew she deserved better.

Someone gently tapped on Warren's door. When Warren answered the door, he found one of Pierce's employees with a server of fresh coffee.

"I am alright," Warren advised the server. "You need not worry about me.

"Oh no, Mr. McKinley," the small framed bald black gentleman replied. "Mr. Pierce say dey ain't nuttin too good for his nephew. Mr. McKinley, I didn't know that you was of relation to Mr. Pierce."

"I reckon so," replied Warren. "Thanks for the coffee."

"Oh," the gentleman snickered. "Taint just coffee. Hit be Mexican coffee. Hit got a smidgen of rum in it. Yes sir."

Warren smiled with acceptance as he grabbed the coffee server.

"Well I do believe I could use a night cap," Warren said.

Warren pulled off his top shirt leaving only his undershirt on and kicked off his shoes. He then half way lay across the tall bed and began to write:

Dearest Melanie,

I have committed to do a foolish thing. Perhaps it isn't quite so foolish for our family's land will be deeded back upon my completion of this project. I realize my untimely schedules have been unfair to you over the years of our marriage and am so sorry to have put you through it all. You never complained but I have taken for granted how lucky I am to have your support in life.

This my dear shall be my last foolish scheme or venture to embark upon. It is perhaps the riskiest thing I have ever done. I know I will be O.K. though for I too much want to return to you.

I have written this letter to you because the words do not come that easy and Thomas was telling me the other day I should write things out that seem to bother me. Thomas seems to have played quite a part in all of our lives lately.

As for my choosing to set out on such a mission as I am doing now, well I cannot lie. I am so in hopes it will resolve the hard feelings between Jack and me. By the time you read this letter, you will already know my outcome. Providing everything goes right, you can expect to see me around a whole lot more. Thank you so very much.

Love,
Warren

Upon completion of writing the letter, Warren sealed it in an envelope and placed a stamp upon it. He then poured another cup of the Mexican Coffee. Just as he was savoring the mixture of java and rum, another tap fell upon his door.

"I don't need anything else, thank you," Warren called out.

"Open the door, Warren," someone called.

The voice sounded much like that of Jack McKinley. Warren knew however that would be very unlikely. He then became very alarmed. If it was Jack, what might he want?

Warren quickly went to the door and asked, "Who is it?"

"It's me, Warren. Jack," his brother replied. "Let me in."

At once, Warren McKinley opened the door and saw his brother standing there. Jack looked much more alert and confident than he did earlier that day. In fact, he looked more like the Jack McKinley, Warren used to know.

"What are you doing Jack?" Warren asked.

Jack smiled at Warren and replied, "You came to Suwannee County for me today. Now I came here for you, brother."

Needless to say, Warren stared at Jack in disbelief. Jack was not supposed to know what he was doing and furthermore he did not expect so many years of intense dislike to end so quickly and easily.

"I do not understand," a skeptical Warren admitted.

"I talked with Sam Pierce," Jack said. "He told me why you gambled away the place Warren. I hated you for so many years simply because you were only trying to do something for me. I was wrong, Warren," Jack continued as he began choking up. "Can you ever forgive me, although I was too little a person to forgive you?"

Warren also choked up as he accepted Jack with open arms. It was for that moment Warren had long awaited. When they were kids, Jack was Warren's hero and nothing had changed. For it was a dream come true for Warren McKinley.

Jack and Warren both accepted blame for the years of useless anguish they had spent and the years of happiness they had deprived their family of having.

"Things will be different," Jack promised.

Finally the two men celebrated their truce with Mexican Coffee. Warren explained to Jack his intent of spending more time with Melanie and at last a somber look overcame Jack.

"After leaving the home place today, I wound up over there where Sam Pierce was having them clear out. Sam told me about the nitro, Warren," Jack said.

"What all did he tell you?" Warren asked.

"Oh, I think he told me everything, Warren. Are you planning on flying it to the gulf in the morning."

"Dead Man's Bay to be exact," Warren admitted as he gently swallowed a gulp of coffee.

"I want to help you," Jack said.

"Thank you, Jack," Warren replied. "It is my responsibility though."

"You are going to need someone to steady the cargo in case of turbulence while you fly," Jack commented.

"I'll cushion it so everything will be O.K.," Warren said.

"Please let me help," Jack finally said with a pleading smile.

Warren didn't have to reply. The handshake was good enough for the two brothers. A deal had been made and they would both sleep a little sounder just having their differences resolved.

Chapter XXVI

Melanie McKinley's slumber was interrupted during the twilight hours of the eventful morning by an incoming shrimp boat. She got out of bed and looked out the cottage's window toward the river. After stretching and yawning she prepared for that day that would determine the fate of her husband.

Once Melanie was dressed and her hair was combed out, she waltzed on over to the large bungalow of James and Martha McKinley. She went inside through the kitchen door and put on coffee. She began mixing flour up for biscuits and then cracked eggs.

Soon thereafter, Melanie was joined by Martha and James McKinley. They all exchanged the ritual good morning's and sat down to a cup of coffee.

Melanie, the last of the three was being seated when Thomas walked into the kitchen.

"Good morning Mr. Wheeler," Melanie said. "Have a cup of coffee."

"I think I'll carry Amos out a cup and be back in a minute," the young man replied.

"You sure do take care of that Amos don't you?" Martha asked rhetorically as James and Melanie chuckled.

"Yea, it's a full time job," grumbled Thomas through an increasing smile. "Somebody has to do so I reckon it might as well be me."

"Before you go, Thomas," Melanie said. "I just needed to say something to all of you."

"Oh," Martha replied.

Melanie then hung her head as if she had something to be ashamed of. "Yes," she began. "I am sorry about the way I acted last night."

"Aw, honey," Martha said, "there is nothing to be sorry about. You did nor said a thing out of line."

"Well," Melanie stated, "I wanted to marry Warren McKinley and this is all just part of being his wife." With a mixture of weeping laughter she added, "I guess it's all part of being a McKinley, huh?"

"Well it shouldn't be," James said. "But I reckon it is. Now you don't worry. Everything is going to be alright."

Thomas meandered on out to Amos' quarters with a cup of coffee in hand for each of them. Upon reaching Amos' door, the young man kicked it a couple of times to be granted entry.

"Well, well, look a here," Amos said with a grin. "You remembered old Amos this mornin' after all now didn't ya?"

"Yep," Thomas replied with his million dollar smile. "We fixin' to go home, Amos. We can get them potatoes dug when we get there."

"The first thing we gonna do is get us one of them there bird sandwiches from Miss Ruby's," Amos advised.

"Yea," said Thomas. "I think we need to go to Mason's too."

"Uh huh," Amos replied as he nodded his head with a suspicious look. "You needin' to buy somethin' or just see somebody?" He asked.

Quickly changing the subject, Thomas asked, "Warren going to make it?"

"He's a McKinley ain't he?" Amos replied rhetorically.

Thomas smiled profoundly in regards to his old buddy's reassuring answer. The young man was maturing enough to realize it was his friend Amos he could always turn to for optimism and honesty. He was also mature enough to know that Amos didn't care as much for the bird sandwiches as he just wanted to see Miss Ruby.

"It's still going to be a gut wrenching wait for the folks though," Amos advised. "You need to be strong for 'em, Thomas Wheeler."

"I know," Thomas admitted. "I know."

Thomas Wheeler returned to the bungalow where he and his family members would anxiously await the charming hum of the Continental engine from behind the cowling of Warren McKinley's Piper Cub.

As the McKinley's and Wheeler's waited to hear the bellow of the little plane, Jack and Warren were very carefully placing twenty-four cylinders of clear liquid inside the storage area of the small cub. Warren remained inside the plane as Jack carefully handed him one cylinder at a time. At last, all cylinders were aboard and the fly boys were ready for takeoff.

Sam Pierce strolled out near the plane. Nobody was permitted to go nearby as they loaded their combustible cargo.

"Now boys," Sam warned, "ya'll are going to have to be extremely careful. The slightest jolt will blow the whole plane and anything around it sky high and all to pieces. You boys sure ya'll still want to go through with this."

"We're sure," Warren said confidently as he pulled a sealed and stamped envelope from inside his vest. "You mind dropping this in the mail?"

"Just in case," Sam Pierce commented.

"I want it mailed regardless," Warren stated.

"Good luck," Sam said as he exchanged handshakes with both Warren and Jack.

The McKinley brothers climbed aboard the airplane after Warren gave it a final preflight inspection and cranked it up. In no time at all, they were taxiing down the runway.

The sun appeared to be a giant orange emerging from the Atlantic Ocean as they quickly gained altitude. Warren leveled it out at eight thousand feet and they flew at about sixty-five knots in a west, south westerly direction.

Jack was not at all skeptical of Warren's piloting skills but chose to get a few things off his chest just in case.

"Warren," Jack said, "I have not been much of a brother and if we make it, I'm going to make it up to you."

Warren smiled and replied, "You have already been more of a brother than most guys have and we are going to make it. Just a little warning though, I am not happy with the clouds ahead. They indicate extreme wind shifts. Double check the cargo, we're going to drop a thousand feet."

Jack complied with the directions of his younger brother. He insured the nitro was in position and as Warren gently descended the craft, Jack insured the cargo held in it's place.

The most difficult thing about the entire situation was the limited size of the fuselage and Jack's large frame. There was barely enough room for him to fit into the tiny plane's fuselage, let alone completely turn around and shift dangerous cargo.

The entire flight consisted of just such. It was a constant increase and descent of altitude so that Warren could dodge areas he feared to be turbulent. In fact, he had intentionally veered off course a couple of times just so he could avoid such areas.

At last, the Gulf of Mexico was in sight. The sun was well up into the sky and a glob of threatening clouds could already be seen hovering over the gulf waters.

"That looks scary up ahead," commented Warren, "but we'll be set down before they reach us."

Jack nodded as his nerves continued to wear thinner. Both men were anxious to complete the flight but they had to reach their destination first. Within a few minutes, they could easily see the Steinhachee River. Shortly thereafter, the landing strip was in sight.

Warren maneuvered the cub beyond the airstrip and circled over the Bay Fish Camp where the brothers could see several Wheeler's and McKinley's alike outside waving. Warren looked at his big brother and winked in confidence.

Decreasing the throttle and drastically dropping in altitude, Warren pointed his craft directly to the landing strip where Donavon

Brantley awaited their arrival. Donavon removed his worn captain's hat and held it toward the sun so that he could better see as the plane cleared him by only about twelve feet. Donavon smiled as he rubbed his gruff face and the gentle coastal breeze blew through his long hair.

Finally Donavon watched Warren McKinley guide the plane downward until the wheels touched the grassy runway. The landing was perfect and the little plane rolled to a relatively smooth stop. For a few minutes, Jack and Warren remained in the plane. By the time they got out, the entire family was driving up.

Donavon Brantley sauntered over to the airplane carrying a wooden box and smiled at the McKinley brothers.

"Jack, Warren," Donavon said as he lit a Lucky Strike cigarette. "It's sure good to see you fellows."

"Hello Donavon," Jack replied. "It's awful good for us to see you, too."

"How are we going to get this stuff to your boat?" Warren asked Donavon as he pointed toward the storage area of the plane.

"If you will just hand it to me out of the plane, I'll take it from there," Donavon advised.

Very carefully, Warren removed the cylinders from the cub one by one and handed them to Jack. Jack in turn handed them to Donavon who did not appear to be as careful. Donavon placed all the cylinders in the wood box he had carried. Once the plane was unloaded, Warren got back out of the aircraft and he and Jack smiled at one another.

As James drove closer, Martha focused on her sons. The moment was most rewarding for the senior McKinley's as they witnessed their two sons hug one another. Warren then looked at the two approaching McKinley and Wheeler filled vehicles and gave them all a thumbs up as Jack patted him on the back.

Everyone rushed out of the vehicles and rushed over to Jack and Warren as Martha stood still in amazement. Her bottom jaw remained dropped as she attempted to steady her shaking hands upon her cheeks. She did not attempt to fight back her tears of joy.

Melanie did not say a word. She quietly ran to her husband and held him for a moment. Warren softly comforted her as he promised never again to put her through such.

"Uncle Jack?" Thomas called out in amazement. "I didn't expect to see you," he added with that trademark Wheeler grin.

"Well here I am," Jack replied with a smile of his own. "You didn't think I was going to let Warren do the job without me did you?"

James smiled with such pride as his sons had finally pulled together. He then looked over at Martha who continued to trickle tears of joy.

"Ma," Jack said.

"Come here, Jack McKinley," Martha replied as Jack hugged his mother. "Welcome back son. Welcome back."

"I think there is a pot of coffee waiting for the McKinley Brothers," Rose commented. "Why don't we all go to the house and drink it?"

For the first time in many years, the entire McKinley family was in agreement. Everyone began walking to the automobiles when James informed them he would be remaining there for a short while but would soon be home.

Once the automobiles pulled away, James looked at Donavon and smiled.

"I told Sam I would pay you," James said.

"Pay me for what?" Donavon replied.

"Your time is important," James stated.

Donavon smiled at James and shook his head. "Mr. McKinley," he said, "you do not owe me a thing. I was just glad to do it."

"Well it looks like it worked," James confessed.

"You going to tell them?" Brantley asked.

"No," James quickly replied as he removed one of the cylinders and tossed it in the air. "I want them to think they have really done something. Besides, Martha would kill me if she knew I had put everyone through this for water," he added with a chuckle.

Donavon Brantley joined James McKinley in laughter as they stared at the box full of pure water.

"Anytime I can do anything for you, Mr. McKinley, just let me know," Donavon said as he waved good bye and strolled toward the river.

"Thanks again, Donavon Brantley," James replied and began his walk home knowing that Donavon would never reveal this endeavor having been bogus due to his noble character.

Chapter XXVII

Times of old, lost times, and plans of the future were all discussed among the McKinley-Wheeler dinner later that day. Happiness flowed abundantly throughout the gulf coast bungalow as the celebration lunch was held.

Martha McKinley prepared a scrumptious meal that particular day. The menu offered absolutely everything anyone in their right mind could ever want. Oyster stew and soda crackers.

During lunch Warren commented, "I cannot believe you put up no more opposition than you did to our flying the nitro, Father."

James simply replied, "I knew everything was going to work out." He then looked at Martha and winked while flashing a mischievous grin she was no stranger to.

She then knew the truth and had never been prouder of James McKinley. True, he had created much fear for the entire family. But looking at her sons eating side by side it had all been worthwhile.

Soon after the meal everyone would make an attempt to return to what they perceived as normal lives. Charles and Rose would at last return home as a whole family. Christmas would soon be celebrated then all of the children could return to school. Warren would remain closer to home and legitimate business. As for James and Martha, they would probably be spending a little more time in Suwannee County.

Jack had business in Florida's panhandle for Charles had obviously accepted his deal. Therefore, Jack McKinley had one more journey of truth to embark upon. Stella deserved that. Jack McKinley knew that his love for Stella would be strong enough to bring her home. He knew he had to do that before his deal was made with Charles. Thomas had forced him to face reality even before Charles' return home.

Thomas had just one more errand to run before his journey back to the farm. He walked down to the bait and tackle shop where he had seen some earrings and a matching necklace. The jewelry had been made of seashells and each time he saw the set, he thought of Penelope.

As the young man dandily walked back to the fish camp, his mind drifted. He thought of all the recent turns of events. A certain realization came about him that in life changes and adversity would be inevitable. He had however discovered that no journey would be impossible with a family like his by his side.

When he returned, Amos stood there awaiting him. Thomas smiled and thanked God for being blessed with such a friend and mentor.

Amos was packing some tobacco in the bowl of his pipe as he leaned against the hood of Jack's Ford Coupe. Peacefully he gazed down toward the river and then lit his pipe.

"Amos," Thomas called out. "When we get home, what you say we go into town and get one of them bird sandwiches from Miss Ruby. And while we're there we'll get some laying mash. Them chickens will be quit laying if we don't."

"I expect we'd better," Amos replied as the two best friends walked to the room Amos had occupied to retrieve his few belongings.